BOB MOFFETT'S
POWER PACK 2

BOB MOFFETT'S
POWER PACK 2

SCRIPTURE UNION
130 City Road, London EC1V 2NJ

Printed in Great Britain at The Bath Press, Bath, Avon.
Typeset by Central Typesetting Service Ltd, London EC1Y 8RQ

Design by Tony Cantale Graphics

Artwork and cover illustration by Simon Jenkins

CONTENTS

Preface

'Power Pack 2' is here at last!

Why has it taken so long? Well, I only write one creative idea a month for 'Buzz' magazine, under the title of 'Power Page'!

This book has been published to share some of this teaching for youth groups; creative ideas which will enable young people to understand more about their faith.

Gill Smith has done a fantastic job editing my article each month. She normally receives it two days after the deadline and processes it so fast and efficiently that it always appears on time! Jilly, my wife, the real brains behind the operation, takes my ideas, vets them and then does a superb job of processing them at our end. So to Jilly and Gill, thank you.

So, here they are – for you to adapt and enjoy, so long as you give prayerful and careful consideration to their use. Youth are too important to God for us to let him, and them, down.

Bob Moffett

Introduction

How often do you go out for a slap-up five course meal? Once a week? Once a month? Very occasionally? Just imagine how ridiculous it would be if you depended entirely on those meals to keep you going, and spent the long periods in between fasting.

Yet for so many Christians in Britain, that is the extent of their spiritual diet. They fill themselves to bulging point at church conferences, house-parties and special teaching weeks – then rely on snacks and nibbles until the next biblical banquet comes along.

This series is intended to be a menu card for Christians in that kind of situation. Maybe you go back to your church after a mouth-watering feast, with a big appetite to learn more about God's plan for your life, only to go hungry because there is no planned diet to satisfy you.

Thirty-six of Bob Moffet's 'Power Pages', originally published in 'Buzz' magazine, are reprinted in the original 'Power Pack'. Now, as a result of popular demand, here are twenty-five more!

Their aim is to provide small groups of young people, interested in studying together around the Bible, with a fresh, down-to-earth approach. The studies won't always give all the answers, but will attempt to stimulate the group's thinking on subjects which directly affect their daily lives.

However, these studies are not intended to replace an existing church Bible Study group if there is one already. They are essentially for Christians without a group at present, but may also be used effectively as a supplement to an existing study programme.

In contrast to the first 'Power Pack', the ideas here are not split into two sections. Instead, there is enough material in each idea for you to choose to split it as you like, for study over two or more weeks – maybe adding in your own ideas. If you wish to use an outline for one week only, you may find you want to miss some parts out in order to spend longer on others. Be wise in your deliberations! Don't miss out all the Bible studies or the bits that take time to prepare!

No two groups are the same and each will need to adapt the basic framework to suit its own needs. Time spent in preparation beforehand, both by leaders and the other members, will be invaluable.

GOD, ME
AND
OTHERS

1 *Participation*

'Lord, I want to serve you. I want to be a pawn to be moved around at the will of the grand master of this world. I want to be the spade which the gardener, God, pushes into the soil wherever he likes. I want to be a tool in your service, O Lord. Amen.'

How often have you heard a prayer like that?

It's true we are called to be humble (James 4:10). We are also called to be servants (Romans 6:22 calls us to be slaves to God). But we have also been called the CHILDREN of God (John 1:12). How do we cope with the apparent paradox?

I think the key to the answer is PARTICIPATION.

Participation Games

Prepare your meeting using two out of the three crowdbreaker games below:

1. Blind . . . fold/feed

Arrange couples around a small table and blindfold each player. Plates of feeding mixture are placed on the table between each couple, and every player is equipped with a spoon. On the signal to start each couple begins feeding each other from their own spoon, the winners being the first couple to empty their plate. Make sure their clothes are adequately protected and warn against wild movements of the spoons as this can result in broken teeth. If possible, use plastic spoons. An offer of a shampoo sachet is often very welcome!

Variation: Have each couple cleaning each other's teeth.

2. Bosses and secretaries

Arrange players into couples, with each of the partners at opposite sides of the room. Use all the walls

so that the players are spaced around the room. One member of each pair (the boss) is given a prepared newspaper cutting (use six different messages of approximately the same length), while the other member (secretary) has a piece of paper and a pencil. On the signal to start, the bosses begin dictating the contents of the newspaper cutting to the secretaries who try to take it down. This is a difficult task with so many competing voices. The first couple with a complete, correct message of dictation are the winners.

3. Back to back

Teams are made up, each of two players who stand back-to-back with their arms linked. On the signal to start they run towards a line, one running backwards, the other forwards. As soon as they touch the line they start back, reversing positions.

Variation: Ask the players to try this sideways or get them to start by getting up from the floor in their back-to-back positions.

Involve as many people in your preparation and planning as possible. Discuss with your senior members your ideas and objectives for the evening and how they could be involved.

● **NB.** This may be the ideal opportunity to begin to involve others in leadership, ie. participation.

Begin your activities with the crowdbreakers giving maximum attention to maximum participation. Get your team of helpers to wear boiler suits or bowler hats or anything else to suggest work and togetherness.

Explain to your group that God is not in the business of using us like garden tools. God sees us as co-workers with him.

Read 2 Corinthians 6:1 to the group. God doesn't bypass our minds and intellects. Some people act as if they haven't got brains when it comes to discovering how God wants to involve them – it's as if they believe God has just given them a head to keep their ears apart! No, God wants us to participate in his great adventure.

Research Assignments

Split the group into a number of units with your leaders heading up these units. They should seek to get as many as possible in their unit to answer some of the important questions listed below the assignments. Each unit should only be given one Bible passage, which you should select.

Feedback

Produce a list of the general findings on a flip chart or overhead projector. The overwhelming evidence will suggest that God doesn't treat us as robots with an enormous silicon chip already programmed to move and act in accordance with his pre-recorded electronic signals. No, we participate with him in his world.

Finally

Produce a list of the recognised organisations which are active (or otherwise) in your area – political, social, charitable, educational, uniformed organisations, etc., and challenge your group to participate with God by getting involved with such a group.

● **NB. Health Warning:** Not to participate will mean stagnation; to participate will mean casualties! Jesus took the latter road and lost Judas.

Participation

Research assignments

The call of Abraham	
Abraham and Lot	Genesis 12
Jacob	Genesis 13
Joseph	Genesis 32
Joseph	Genesis 41:39-49
The commission	Genesis 42
Peter's vision	Mark 16:9-20
Council at Jerusalem	Acts 10:9-48
	Acts 15:1-21

Questions

● What part does God have with the personalities involved?
● Who is making the necessary decisions in the narrative?
● How is God functioning with the people involved?
● What is God saying to us about the way he works with us?

2

The 'Tator' family

New Christians are babies in Christ. They have just been 'born again'. They will be enthusiastic to start moving on in their faith and will expect us to help them.

My experience suggests, though, that they will probably make us insecure by their enthusiasm. They will also make a number of mistakes.

Both are exciting in themselves because they are signs of growth. Let's look at how we can grow together in Christ.

INTRODUCTION
The poTATOR Family
Explain that God's family attracts all types of characters and personalities. They have joined the potator family.

With that, tip a bag of potatoes onto the floor (put a plastic sheet down first). It is useful if the potatoes have been scrubbed a little!

Ask members of your group to pick up a potato each. Make a side comment about the fact that there is a 'TATOR' psychology. 'I wonder why you picked that one up, Simon?'

Action
Split people up into groups of five. Ask them to make a list of the TATOR family they know – with descriptions. Before they throw the TATORS at you, believing that you've gone NANAS, explain to them what you want, by giving a couple of examples:

● **Speck TATOR** – Speck is someone who prefers watching other people do things. He always seems to have plenty of advice and is often shouting it from the sidelines!

● **Hesi TATOR** – Hesi is someone who doesn't make up her mind very easily. She seems to take a lot of time before coming to a decision. When she does, it is probably well thought out even if it's too late!

Give your groups paper and pens and ask them for some creative and original thinking.

Here are a few more examples if you really need to help any of the groups.

DICK Tator   DEVAS Tator
AGI Tator   VEGI Tator
IMMY Tator   IRRI Tator
MEDI Tator   COMMON Tator
COGI Tator

Give them 13 minutes to do this. Afterwards, ask each group leader in rotation to read out one name. Highlight the exhaustive list on a flipchart or overhead projector. Keep this section reasonably jovial.

Talk about God's TATOR family. With new Christians, welcome them into it. Without taking the illustration too far you can talk about our being put in the pot together. God keeps his eye upon us and drops in the additives to make us a little more appetising, etc.

As members of God's family there are responsibilities that we all need to take seriously. Let us look at some of these together in our groups.

Although I have given verses with the headings, you may wish to list the verses separately on cards for each group, so that they discover the 'responsibilities' for themselves.

● **Praying for each other**
Ephesians 6:18-20
James 5:16
● **Sharing the family's faith with others**
Acts 1:8
● **Loving one another**
John 13:34,35
Hebrews 13:1,2
● **Forgiving one another**
Matthew 18:21,22
● **Serving one another**
Galatians 5:13-16
1 Peter 4:9,10
● **Looking after each other**
Romans 12:13
● **Being patient with one another**
Ephesians 4:2,3

THE GROUP

WELCOME

Conclusion

You may choose to sum up in the following way: 'One of the ways God's family "mashes" together is through corporate prayer, when people feel free to pray for one another – their needs, their families, their joys, etc.

'We are going to do that right now. We are going to pray round in a circle. I would encourage all of you to pray out loud just one, simple, specific prayer.

'Just a one-sentence prayer will do. I will begin and then pass a Bible to the next person in the circle. If you want to pray, hold on to it until you have finished, then pass it on to the next person. If you don't want to pray pass the Bible on.'

After the prayers, encourage them to pray simply and read their Bible during the next week. Without it they will starve and fade away. Have available a selection of Bible reading notes for their particular age group. I strongly recommend that you have *JAM* magazine available if your group are early to middle teenagers (can be obtained from Christian bookshops or Herald House Ltd., 27 Chapel Road, Worthing, Sussex BN11 1EG).

Whatever you hand out, do not charge for the material. Your church should back your ministry on this occasion.

3

Little boxes, people boxes

Whenever I go anywhere people are always wanting to put me in a 'box'. Not that they want to get rid of me – rather, they want to put me into a particular 'safe' category in their thinking.

Is he married? Has he got any children? What does he do when not working? What's he really like? Is he really only 26?

To answer these: Yes, I'm married to Jill, and we have two daughters, Tanya and Amy. The other questions I'm not going to answer!

But we all – consciously or unconsciously – put people in boxes, and in doing so we often make big mistakes about people.

With this page of ideas we are going to try to understand our façades as well as our real selves.

Preparation

Buy . . . borrow . . . or steal (borrow for an indefinite period of time), the cassette – titled: *Waiting for Goddard* under the Kingsway label

(KMC 310). Play the song *Child of My Time* and ask your youth group what the basic problem of this sad story was.

Try to draw out from them the fact that we all pigeon-hole people by the way they act and look.

PS. As the youth leader, play this song over and over again before the evening to appreciate its insight.

Action

Divide the group into two. Give each group a large piece of paper and give them the following instructions.

One group (you decide) should draw a caricature of someone who is really 'cool' – someone who is really 'in touch'.

The other group should draw someone who is the opposite of 'cool' – the caricature of the person who they just don't want to look like!

Give them nine minutes to do this.

Hang both pictures up, side by side, unfurling each one slowly for maximum impact. Once the laughter has died down try and list some of the characteristics of the 'cools' and the 'not-so-cools'. Divide your group into two again and give them four minutes to list some of the reasons why they veer towards wanting to be 'cool'.

Read with them three out of four of the following passages:
● Luke 18:15-17; ● 18:18-30;
● 19:1-10; ● 19:35-43; and briefly discuss the way Jesus reacted to different types of people.

Boxes ... boxes ... boxes and more boxes

Before your meeting, arrange for a couple of your youth group to raid your local shops for boxes – they need to be reasonably small but not necessarily all the same size. One will be for each person. Pile them in the middle of the floor along with thousands of magazines (well, a good number anyway), Sellotape, glue and scissors.

Ask each person to take a box and plaster the outside of it with pictures that express how they would like other people to see them.

On the inside of the box, including the lid, they should stick pictures to show how they see themselves – so that the inside reflects 'the real me', and the outside reflects 'the way I want others to see me'.

Finally, ask them to get into groups wih their close friends and show each other their boxes, explaining the reasoning behind their collages both inside and out.

Read to close: Romans 12:1,2, explaining that we are to be continually transformed by the renewing of our minds. It is only the world that puts us into 'boxes'.

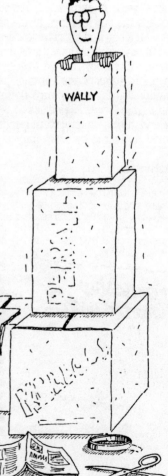

4 Friendship without labels

Two story books we read to our children contain the lines 'The princess was looking for a gay prince' and 'He was a queer fellow'.

Obviously the books were written before the words 'gay' and 'queer' carried the connotations they do now. What's more, now that we have such words, people are quick to apply them as labels to relationships between people of the same sex. Close friendships between people of the opposite sex don't escape the labelling syndrome either.

If a boy and a girl have a deep friendship and share their fears, joys and plans with each other they are seen as 'going steady'. If two boys or two girls spend much time together and love and support one another, people suspect they have tendencies the wrong way. Neither may be the case.

This Power Page looks at friendship without labels; friendship as an important quality for its own sake and an art to be cultivated by everyone.

Activities

Begin by giving each member of your group a card and pen and ask them to devise a twenty-word advertisement seeking a friendship with a member of the same sex and age group. Each advertisement should begin with:

Friendship
wanted with...

Read out any appropriate adverts you can find in the personal columns of selected newspapers and magazines.

Give them four minutes to do this and then call the cards in and read out a selection. In the normal Power Page style the writers remain anonymous.

As you read out the cards have someone list the positive qualities which we look for in friendship, which may have been expressed in the advertisements. Hopefully you pull out some of the following:

- Friendly
- Helpful
- Trustworthy
- Sensitive
- Understanding
- Encouraging
- Honest
- Open
- Forgiving
- Sharing
- Listening
- Peaceful
- Humorous
- Loyal

Give each of the qualities listed a letter and then write these letters on a blank card. Place these cards face down on the floor. Each person in turn picks up a card and is asked a question from the box entitled: 'Positive Questioning'. If, for example, a person picks up card 'D' he would have to answer the question 'D' in the list.

If you have more people than qualities just add a few more cards and leave them blank – adds to the excitement and tension! Please make sure that answers are of a general nature as it could be an embarrassment if they were too specific.

Positive Questioning

A Why do you call a certain person your 'best' friend?
B Give one way in which you have been helpful to a friend.
C Why is trust so important in friendship?
D Give one incident where a friend showed you sensitivity.
E Give one example as to how you recently showed understanding to a friend.
F Define 'encouragement'.
G How easy is it to be honest with a friend when they may not like what you tell them? Give an example.
H How would you describe somebody who is said to be 'open'?
I Give an example of a time when you expressed forgiveness.
J What is the most important thing you have shared with a friend? – in general terms please.
K Why is it so difficult at times to listen to friends?
L If someone is said to have a peaceful personality what does that mean?
M Someone may have a humorous personality but is that always a good thing?
N What does it mean to have a loyal friend?

SPLIT your group up and give them the following passages on friendship. They should pull out as many aspects of friendship as possible from the texts. Give them twelve minutes to do this.

● **Jonathan befriends David**
1 Samuel 18:1-4
● **Jonathan protects David**
1 Samuel 19:1-7
● **Jonathan helps David**
1 Samuel 20:11-23
● **The friends of the paralysed man** Luke 5:17-20
● **Paul and Timothy**
2 Timothy 1:1-7
● **Paul's practical advice on friendship** 1 Corinthians 16:1-12

Finally give each member of your group a 'Personal Friendship Chart' and ask them to circle their rating of friendship. This should be done privately before they go.

Finish with some open prayers on friendship.

Personal Friendship Chart – How friendly am I?

Quality	Poor										Good
Friendly	0	1	2	3	4	5	6	7	8	9	10
Helpful	0	1	2	3	4	5	6	7	8	9	10
Trustworthy	0	1	2	3	4	5	6	7	8	9	10
Sensitive	0	1	2	3	4	5	6	7	8	9	10
Understanding	0	1	2	3	4	5	6	7	8	9	10
Encouraging	0	1	2	3	4	5	6	7	8	9	10
Honest	0	1	2	3	4	5	6	7	8	9	10
Open	0	1	2	3	4	5	6	7	8	9	10
Forgiving	0	1	2	3	4	5	6	7	8	9	10
Sharing	0	1	2	3	4	5	6	7	8	9	10
Listening	0	1	2	3	4	5	6	7	8	9	10
Peaceful	0	1	2	3	4	5	6	7	8	9	10
Humorous	0	1	2	3	4	5	6	7	8	9	10
Loyal	0	1	2	3	4	5	6	7	8	9	10

5

Denominationalism

'C of Epentebaptandcomethacongrefreequake', sings the effervescent *Ishmael* in an astute little ditty on the increasing number of different types of churches.

There are other categories too – house church, established church, free church, independent church, exclusive church . . .

They're all nothing more than labels really, used to express an identity. But there is a tendency to put the various church types into a worship league table.

But it's not as easy as that. Even when those who are dissatisfied with their own particular worship move out of their traditional settings to a house or free church they can often be disappointed to find that it, too, can become staid and dull.

Any church that is not constantly changing and moving with God's direction is, of necessity, a dead church in spite of the label.

In the end it's not the form of worship or what kind of spiritual 'experience' you've had that matters so much as whether the church is following God's call to move forward. Are we listening to his voice and co-operating as he moves the church on?

Action

Prepare a sheet of all the road signs that are known to you (purchase a copy of the *Highway Code*). You can do this by sketching them on a sheet and photocopying or duplicating a sheet for each person.

Every member of your group should make comments about his feelings on his church by making use of some of the printed road signs, eg. underneath a roundabout sign, he may write 'CHURCH GOING ROUND IN CIRCLES'. A bumpy road sign might be used to mean 'CHURCH

GOING THROUGH AN UNEASY TIME'.

Think up your own examples, making sure they're relatively humorous but that, at the same time, they also make their point.

Give your group 14 minutes to write the captions under the signs then go round asking what everyone

put. Ask them specifically why they made their comments and try to get to the roots of their thinking. Allow them to be honest even if any negativism makes you feel insecure.

Make a list of their comments.

WARNING:
SHEPHERDING
SYSTEM IN
OPERATION

Talk

The church is far from perfect – that's why Christ came. God saw that all was not 'hunky dory' and decided on the radical move of sending his son to this world.

'The church is a hospital for sinners, not a rest home for saints.' Paul would not have written so many letters to the churches in the New Testament if they had been perfect. A church is a family and, like all families, has its ups and downs.

But the family of God should be pulling together, respecting each member's gifts and personality, even if it can't always agree on everything.

Read with the group 1 Corinthians 12:12-26 and then tell them they are going to do an exercise.

WARNING:
CONCEALED
BAPTISTRY
NOW IN USE

WARNING:
BILLY GRAHAM-
STYLE APPEALS
LIKELY

Simulation game

Black out the room where you are having your meeting and establish an element of intrigue.

They are to play a simulation activity that will highlight the importance of co-operation and will also encourage teamwork in your group.

You will need

● eight pieces of paper
● a torch
● a candle and
● a box of matches.

Before the players arrive:
● place the torch in a prominent place
● hide the candle in the room
● hide the empty matchbox and
● hide the matches.

Give each player a folded piece of paper on which is written the role they must play in the game. If you have more than eight people, split into teams and repeat the game for each team. The others will have to leave the room.

Explain the rules of the game:
1. The object is to get some light into the room.
2. No one may speak except the speaker, but the speaker may ask people direct questions to which they can reply.
3. No one may move except the helper and those whose role gives them certain limited movement.
4. The game ends when the candle is lit.

Tell everyone to read their roles silently, then turn out the lights. The following roles are found on the eight pieces of paper:
● You are the speaker. You have the ability to speak but you may not move.
● Only you have the ability to hold candles. You may move but only when you are holding a candle.
● Only you have the ability to hold a matchbox. You may move only when holding a matchbox.
● There is a matchbox hidden (give location).
● You have the ability to use the torch. You may do nothing else. You may move anywhere, but not until someone gives you a torch.
● There is a candle hidden (give location).
● There are some matches hidden (give location).
● You are a helper. You may move anywhere but you may not speak to anyone (not even the speaker). You may carry objects from one place to another but you may not use them.

The easiest way to begin is for the speaker to address each player and have them reveal their role. The game will flow naturally from there until the candle is lit.

Discuss 1 Corinthians 12:12-26 again in light of this exercise.

Old folk

They tottered past the house every night as they held each other up on the way home from the local pub.

It was not that they were drunk, but just old. It was not that they had nothing else to do than sit in the corner downing one or two pints, but it was the only place that they met other people.

It was not that they were well liked down at the local, but they were always there and you had to be friendly and make polite conversation about the weather or Bert's only other interest – growing leeks.

One night they didn't arrive. The landlord made passing comments to two or three of his locals about the vacant corner.

No one really seemed to worry. Four weeks later the locals read the sad story of an elderly couple who had died of hypothermia (lack of heat).

At the local no one put two and two together to realise it was the same couple. It was six months later, at closing time that the landlord paused as he shut the door and wondered where 'that' elderly couple had gone; but it was only a passing thought as the pub had recently become very popular amongst the young professionals – more spending power!

Thirteen per cent of the population in this country is elderly compared with only 3.5 per cent in Brazil and 6 per cent in India. More and more of our financial resources are taken up in providing care for the elderly, particularly in the area of medical and social services.

It is a sad comment upon us that, even so, we do not take 'the aged' seriously, either in caring for them or treating them as responsible and wise members of our community.

Action
Read or (better) photocopy the scenario of the elderly couple above and ask your group to make a list of all the words that come to their mind as they read the story. They should write these down on the left hand side of a blank piece of paper.

Once they have done that, ask them to express in a few words what they feel or think about the story. (Their thoughts should correspond to the words in their list.)

Organise your group into smaller units of four or five and ask them to share their lists with one another, resulting in the production of a master list of all the difficulties that the elderly face in our society.

Bring all the units together and write all their ideas down on the left hand side of a flip chart or overhead projector.

Explain that this represents a negative view of the elderly and that we all fall into the trap of thinking about old age in negative terms.

Show how the media reinforces this negative image. The heroes and heroines are the young and active. Fashion and advertisements are geared predominantly to the under 35's. (Illustrate your point with advertisements from magazines and if you want to be really adventurous show numerous TV advertisements on a video recorder.)

Research
The Bible shows a different angle on old age:
1. Think of the many great people who were getting on in age:
● Abraham (Gen. 12:4)
● Moses (Deut. 34:7; Exod. 7:6,7)
● Noah (Gen. 5:32; 7:6).
All of these attained a great age before God called them to their special assignments.

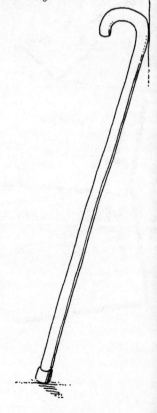

2. The Bible assumes that the elderly will be looked after:
● Exodus 20:12 and Leviticus 19:32 – commands not requests.
● Mark 7:9-12 shows it is hypocrisy to use religion as an excuse for not looking after aged parents.
3. The Bible recalls the faithfulness of the elderly Simeon and Anna in Luke 2:22-38.

Seek from your group the positive aspects of being older and make a list on the right hand side of the same sheet of paper you had used for the negative aspect.

Follow on: Adopt a Granny
We have heard about the 'Help the Aged' organisation. I am suggesting a 'Help the Youth' movement by 'adopting a granny'.

This is sneaky because most young people think that they can help old people but when they take time to regularly visit an older person they discover they learn and receive more than they could ever give.

A Granny Extra
Contact a few of the elderly people in church and ask them to come along to one of your scheduled youth meetings.
On their arrival split your group into smaller units and give the following questions to one of the group to ask of the elderly person(s) designated to sit with them.

How does 'Adopt a Granny' work?

1. Sell the idea of visiting an older person on the basis of what they have discussed from the exercises above.
2. Acknowledge that a lot of younger people are a bit scared of visiting elderly people, because they often appear to act and look strange.
3. Arrange for your group to visit 'pre-arranged' elderly people or couples, in pairs, the week after this meeting, explaining your plan. Start with the church elderly first.
4. They are to make a commitment to visit every fortnight for three months and offer any assistance to them they can.
5. As the youth leader you keep a record of their visits (as a good youth leader you then delegate this responsibility).
6. Arrange with your group a party or concert date so that they work towards bringing their elderly along to something that the youth have arranged.

1. What were things like when you were our age?
2. What was one thing which really helped your growth in Christ?
3. Did you grow up in a Christian family?
4. When did you make a commitment to Christ?
5. Can you give us some suggestions or advice to help us in our faith?
6. What would you do differently if you had the chance?
7. What can we specifically pray about for you, or what concern can we help with?

Scenario — Old Age

Pointless   – what was their life for?
Loneliness – they didn't seem to have any real friends.
Why?   – why didn't someone bother?
Boring   – they did the same thing every night!

'Teenager'

When does your church discuss teenagers? When a snooker ball's smashed a window? When a naughty word has appeared on the toilet wall?

Sadly, the subject of teenagers is brought up in most churches in a forum where teenagers themselves are not present. Our church structures tend to keep the age groups apart.

One of my friends told me recently, 'The young have never been old, but the old have once been young and therefore ought to be more understanding.' I have some sympathy for this view.

Teenagers and their relationship with the rest of the local church is the theme for this session. We'll also be learning how to do a survey of popular opinion in the church.

Objective
To open up or enhance communication between the old and young. The old, here, are defined as anyone over the age of 30!

Options
You have two options. **First**, this could be an activity for the whole church – a special meeting organised by you and your minister/church leader. Sunday afternoon would be a good time and you could lend by having tea together. Or, **secondly**, you could confine the activity to just young people.

The former idea is much better as this could be a very special experience for your whole church.

The latter, although very worthwhile and important, would not have the desired effect as quickly.

Action
I am assuming that the whole church is gathered. However, if it is just your group, you'll have to adapt the instructions.

Before they all take their places read the following (or adapt it to your group): 'This evening (afternoon) we have come to talk together. Please sit in the group to which you feel you belong. Some of you will have a choice of more than one group. For example you could be 24 and married, in which case choose the group you feel suits you.'

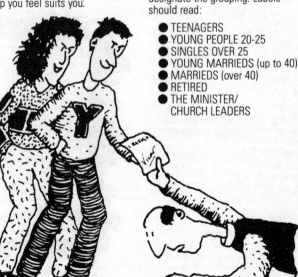

Ask people to do two things very quickly:
1. Elect a group leader.
2. To break the ice, go round the circle asking each person to name one food they like and one they dislike. If anyone wishes to pass, they can do so by saying 'pass'.

Explain that you want each group to write down any questions or messages they may have for any of the other groups. For example, the singles might want the marrieds to invite them around to their homes more often. The teenagers might want to ask church leaders why they can't have more say in worship.

Arrange for refreshments prior to the start, with the young people serving drinks. This is good psychology! Put out chairs in circles around the room/hall beforehand with a large label for each circle to designate the grouping. Labels should read:

- TEENAGERS
- YOUNG PEOPLE 20-25
- SINGLES OVER 25
- YOUNG MARRIEDS (up to 40)
- MARRIEDS (over 40)
- RETIRED
- THE MINISTER/ CHURCH LEADERS

Important: For any negative comment you make to each of the groups there must be one positive message as well (read Eph. 4:1-6).

Give the groups 25 minutes to work on their messages. If the whole church is gathered, group leaders can deliver the messages to the relevant groups there and then. If you've only got the teenagers there you could send the messages to the groups via the minister.

Finally, each group must prepare a message for the whole church. Give them 6 minutes to do this and then get group leaders to read out the message. Remember the rules: one positive comment for every negative one.

Opinion poll

I suggest you conduct this opinion poll on a separate occasion. The questionnaire should be prepared by your youth group and is intended for all church members, including them. Get your minister's support.

Keep it simple and anonymous, with your youth group preparing most of the questions – although you will have to give some help. Have the questionnaire typed and copied – one for each church member. Below is a very brief and limited example. Amplify it as you wish. Make sure

you get at least 85 per cent of the church members replying.

Arrange for one of your bright ones to work out percentage charts for publication in the church magazine or newsletter. If you don't have one it's back to duplicating.

Important: You may feel that it is going to take a lot of work to carry out these ideas. However, this meeting will probably be one of the most enriching experiences of the year.

To The Vicar
From The teenagers

We think you're great. You talk to us, you know our names and don't ignore us after the service. Although we think you are a lousy pool player, we let you off.

Just one thing does bug us a bit and that is you don't let us play our choruses in the church. Give us a thought when you prepare next Sunday's bonanza.

Pete goes to college

Pete arrived at his pre-arranged college digs.

The ageing couple showed him to a bare room where, except for a bed which seemed to dominate the floor space, the armchair and the rickety table which passed as a desk, there appeared to be little else. His heart sank.

In this outline we are going to tackle the very real dilemma of how to help those who have to move away from home to go to college or perhaps to a new place of work, or maybe even to the mission field.

Sadly, for many who leave home for college or a new job, their initial lot is 'not a happy one'. But things can often get worse as they go along. Let's take up the story of our friend Pete again:

The term started with the normal college 'freshers' activities. Although a sociable character, Pete didn't want to attend some of the late-night fringe activities which appeared to compromise his firm Christian commitment.

Finding himself at one of the deadest churches in town (unplanned), where even the woodworm were asleep, he goes home to his digs feeling very low.

Pete's story could become a sad reality for any Christian leaving home. For this reason we must take our responsibilities seriously when considering those who leave our family to live away. The following simulation game explores ways in which your group can 'keep the home fires burning.'

Action

As everyone arrives, put two of your group (boy and girl) into two separate rooms, eg. one in the kitchen, another in a small bedroom (a bare room!) or a loo.

The rest of your group should go to the normal room for your meeting. Arrange special food, new term, new academic year celebrations. Have some crazy games and loud singing. This should last for 25 minutes before allowing the other two out of their rooms.

Before bringing them into the main body of the group, put the two together giving them time to chat for a few minutes. Give no reason for their confinement except, of course,

that they are helping you with your evening programme. It would be even better if the group as a whole were unaware of their presence in the house until they are brought in.

Ideally you would bring them in at the height of your frivolity and enjoyment, at which point you abruptly cut the whole thing and lead into a serious discussion.

Ask the two from 'outside' the following questions:

1. Did you like being outside by yourself?

2. What thoughts were going on in your mind? Were they particularly pleasant and positive thoughts?

3. Where did you want to be?

4. What did loneliness mean to you in terms of what or who you missed?

Ask the group the following questions asking them to be acutely honest with their comments and answers:
1. What were your feelings when you discovered that they had missed out on all the 'food, fun and fellowship?'
2. How could you have alleviated their loneliness in very practical ways, other than by asking them to join you?

Back to the party
For the next 10 minutes get back into the party swing, with the two 'outsiders' now very much involved. Then again bring it to an abrupt end.

Read Philemon 1-22. With everybody looking at these verses in their own Bible, point out to them that Paul was in prison and that Onesimus, although he had run away from his master, Philemon, was Paul's close companion.

List
Ask your group to prepare a list of ways that they could help anyone, whether they be a college student, someone sent away to work, or a missionary, to feel part of the family of God's church. Unless the group makes very firm arrangements to act upon their list on a regular basis then this exercise will have been worthless. Involving others from the church is also essential so that the whole family participate.

Follow on: If you or your friend is going away to college, arrange in advance for the Christian Union there to contact you or your friend on arrival. Do this by simply copying the following details down onto a postcard or letter and sending it to UCCF, The Universities and Colleges Christian Fellowship of Evangelical Unions.

Please give as much of the following information as possible. The earlier we receive news of new students *(after A level results or a place has been confirmed)* the better we can act to make an effective welcome possible.

NAME (Block letters)_____

HOME ADDRESS _____

Please tick if it would be appropriate to send:

Welcome letter from CU ☐

Starting as a Student (free book from UCCF) ☐

UNIVERSITY or COLLEGE *(College is necessary at Cambridge, Oxford, London and Durham)*

HALL/COLLEGE/DIGS ADDRESS *(important for rapid contact)*

SUBJECT *(if known)*_____

Possible attitude to the Christian Union:

Definitely interested ☐ Possibly interested ☐ Attitude uncertain ☐

Any further information:

(It would be of great help if, in sending information on the above pattern, a separate sheet of paper could be used for each individual.)

Name *(Mr, Miss, Mrs, Dr, Rev)*_____

Address _____

Please send to:

Freshers names,
UCCF
38 De Montfort Street
Leicester LE1 7GP

9

Meekness

(The meek shall inherit the earth . . . if that's OK with the rest of you.)

I grew up with the hymn 'Gentle Jesus meek and mild'. It was one of my favourites at junior school.

This, plus fairy-tale, squeaky-clean picture posters on the walls of the Sunday School classroom, gave me a mental picture of a Jesus who displayed effeminate, weak characteristics and looks.

One felt he spoke with such a soft voice that you needed to be leaning on his recently-shaven chin to even hear the stories he was telling.

Few films have dared to blow this image. Only one which I can remember, Denis Potter's 'Son of Man', which created so much controversy that the media showed it again!

One of the Beatitudes says, 'Blessed are the meek, for they will inherit the earth' (Matthew 5:5). If we take Jesus' words literally, he's telling us to be weak, passive and effeminate – surely a recipe for disaster.

Arrival
As your group arrive greet them playing the part of Charles Dickens' character, Uriah 'your very 'umble servant' Heep. Make sure you play this character way over the top with your extreme "umbleness".

Activities
Arrange for either or both of these crowdbreakers to be played – preferably outside.

1. Make a circle with a radius of seven feet. Place a dozen guys inside it. At a given signal each person tries to push everybody else out of the circle, while trying to stay in himself. Once a guy is pushed out of the circle, he retires from the game. The last person to stay in wins.

● **Variation:** Place all the guys in a circle and have the girls surround it. On the given signal, the girls see how long it takes to push, pull, drag etc. all the guys out from inside the circle. The guys cannot fight back in any way. They can only cling to each other for defence.

2. Players join hands in a circle around a mat. Then, by pulling, pushing and tugging, each player tries to make someone else step on to the mat without doing so himself. Players drop out of the game once they touch the mat. If the circle breaks, the two players who let go must drop out.

● Ask your group to write on a piece of paper (which you have provided) the first few thoughts which come into their minds when they hear the word 'meekness'. After ninety-five seconds have people express what they have written.

● Explain that 'meekness' in the Bible has a double-edged meaning referring to our attitude to God and our attitude to our fellow man. Often the word 'meek' is interchanged with 'gentleness' and humility.

● Make a list of what the Bible says about those who are meek, humble or oppressed, by working through the following verses shown on the chart:

Meekness/Humbleness/Oppressed

Verse	What the Bible says
Psalm 10:17	e.g. The Lord hears them.
25:9	
34:2	
37:11	
69:32	
76:9	
147:6	
Prov. 3:34	
16:19	
Isaiah 11:4	
29:19	

Moses and Jesus were called 'meek'
(Numbers 12:3 and Matthew 11:29).
  Get your group to do some
brainstorming about the character
and personalities of Jesus and
Moses. They undoubtedly exuded
his 'gentle giant' attitude.
  Produce a list of such
characteristics and use this as a
check list for each person, i.e. once
the master list is produced on a
board, each person copies it down
and then puts a tick if they feel they
exercise such qualities themselves.

Personal Check List

Characteristic	Moses	Jesus	Me
Determined			
Self controlled			
Listened to God			
Considerate			
Kind			
Patience			

(Example Only)

AN ALTERNATIVE METHOD OF CLEARING THE CIRCLE

● Read Matthew 26:39,42 to your group.
● Explain that Jesus epitomised the characteristic of meekness throughout his whole life. It was an underlying attitude that is expressed through all the listed characteristics seen in the 'Personal Check List' chart. Galatians 5:22,23 explains the true characteristics of the 'fruit (singular) of the spirit'.

Meekness is strength – something to be desired at all costs.
● To close read Psalm 37:1-11 quietly.

IT HAPPENS TO CHRISTIANS TOO!

10

Persecution

Wherever Christians undergo persecution, the Church seems to grow in both the spiritual and the numerical dimension.

Many centuries ago Tertullian, one of the early Christian fathers, declared: 'The blood of the martyrs is the seed of the Church.' His statement is as accurate for today as it was then. Consider the USSR, for example, and other Iron Curtain countries.

Yet the other week I met someone who is under pressure, mainly because he has rubbed people up the wrong way through his manner of witnessing. He has 'taken on' the martyrdom syndrome and makes it clear he believes he's being persecuted for his Christian faith.

The following ideas take the lid off persecution – and will make us all feel 'got at'!

Action

Decide on a popular colour, for example, red or blue. As people arrive, if they are wearing that colour 'find fault' with them. Bring up something about them that is not too personal and have words. Ask, 'Why do you keep a dog?' 'Why were you late on Sunday?' 'Why don't you talk to others more?'

Keep on 'persecuting' them until everyone has arrived. Be very pleasant to the others (ie. the non-red), offering them coffee and biscuits etc. Then announce your subject and apologise to all those you have been rude to.

Ask for definitions of the word 'persecution' until you get agreement that it is something like: 'being subject to persistent ill-treatment of a physical or mental nature.'

Pass out a number of old mags and newspapers and ask each person to tear out three items – articles, pictures, cartoons etc – that express persecution. The three articles should suggest three different types of persecution:
1. physical
2. mental
3. personal

Give them nine minutes to do this, and with the papers all over the floor, ask each person why they have chosen their particular items. Be careful with the third and give them the option to decline.

Research

Explain that Christians are expected to face persecution. Not that they go looking for it, but when you make a stand it often attracts opposition. Split them into smaller groups and ask them to use the following verses to prepare reasons for 'Christian' persecution: ● Matthew 5:10-12,44; 13:18-21; ● John 5:16; 15:20; ● Romans 8:35.

Explain that sometimes Christians declare that they are being persecuted for their faith when their attitudes and actions towards other people are not particularly pleasant. Some Christians say that their witnessing has led to persecution, when in reality their aggressiveness in talking about Jesus has caused them to be one big 'pain in the neck' wherever they go.

You should never use persecution as a test to gauge whether you are serving the Lord. That very persecution may be a result of manufacturing it in our minds.

Attitudes to persecution vary. But what does the Bible say on the subject? Choose two or three verses: ● Romans 8:35; ● 12:14; ● 2 Corinthians 12:10. Then read the words of Polycarp, the Bishop of Smyrna, as he went to the stake

c.160 AD): **'For 86 years I have been his servant and he has never done me wrong; how can I blaspheme the King who saved me?'**

Follow on

What about those Christians today who are *really* suffering for their commitment to Christ? Read Hebrews 13:3 to the group and explain that it is our duty to support our brothers and sisters who are facing persecution and that we should take practical steps to help relieve their plight. Write to, or telephone, the organisations below for literature and information about ways of helping. Decide what each member is going to do in the way of writing letters, preparing information for wider use in the church – posters, prayer lists, newsletters etc.

KESTON COLLEGE,
Heathfield Road,
Keston,
Kent BR2 6BA

Tel: 0689 50116

OPEN DOORS,
PO Box 6
Standlake,
Witney
Oxon OX8 7SP

Tel: 08673 262

11 *Sin*

Sin is one of those emotive words that we prefer not to hear. It's guaranteed to turn us off immediately. 'Anyway, we have been forgiven – the chorus sheets and the Bible tell us so!' we say.

However, many of us lead pseudo-Christian lives because we attempt to con God and our friends into believing that we're OK and 'going on with the Lord' when we know, and God knows, that we're just living a lie.

Let's drop our guard for a while and spend some time 'looking in' at ourselves, so that we'll be able to 'get out.'

Action

As your group arrives, arrange for a good slide photograph to appear on a screen. This should be a picture of anyone or of a group but you must show it in such a way that it appears distorted on the screen.

Make no comment and carefully watch to see if anyone takes the initiative and adjusts the focus to make the picture clear. If they do, casually adjust the projector to distort the image again.

Once everyone is there, discuss the distorted picture, picking up the frustrations of the group at not being able to see it clearly. Allow this to continue for three of four minutes

and then declare in a slow and emphatic way that your subject is sin. For extra effect, slowly spell it out: S-I-N.

Explain that sin distorts the real 'me'. It spoils our relationships with other people because we see them through a 'me' that is already out of perspective – out of balance with the creator God who made all things perfect.

Research: A question of sin

Divide your group up for a lightning Bible study and give them the following questions and references:
1. Was there sin before the creation of mankind? (Gen. 3:1-4; John 8:44.)

2. What was the subtle lie of the devil that introduced 'sin' into the world? (Gen. 3:5.)
3. Why did the couple suddenly feel naked? (Gen. 3:7.)
4. God curses the serpent, but what is the sting in the tail? (Gen. 3:14-15.)
5. The woman is found guilty of her act. What appears to be her punishment? (Gen. 3:16.)
6. Adam was also found guilty and tried to blame the woman (Gen. 3:12). However, God declares that life for him is to become harder. How? (Gen. 3:17-19.)

Explain that it is very difficult for us to imagine what it must have been like to live in 'perfection' as our thinking has been so blurred by sin. As Niebuhr has said: 'Man's sin lies in his pretension to be God.'

It was through this very act, the initial sin, that the natural worship and adoring love that man once gave to his creator was withheld. It is therefore not unusual that, when someone comes into the experience of knowing the forgiveness of sins, he expresses himself in worship.

Demonstrate what sin can do in a person's life by using an old Greek idea:

● Set a lamp in the middle of the floor; switch it on and turn out the lights. Arrange for some, if not all of your group to stand in a circle with their backs to the light.

As they are looking out from the light what do they see? They see a pale reflection of themselves and others – a shadow of their real selves and of their real potential. The reason – their backs are to the light.

Ask them all to turn clockwise until they stand sideways to the circle, neither looking into the light or into the dark. Explain that some people try to get the best of both worlds by 'enjoying the dark side and yet trying to keep in with the light' – impossible.

Ask them all now to turn towards the light. The light now shines and shows them up to be who they really are – the good, the bad and the ugly.

As they are still standing in the circle, read John 8:12; 9:5; 12:46. Do this slowly in an attitude of prayer, having written the three verses out so that there is no break between each verse.

Invite open prayer as you close.

As an alternative way of introducing this subject . . .

Arrange for your group to try their hand at archery. A local group of archers may exist in your area. Failing that (and not just as an easy option) arrange for a dart board to be set up and give each person in turn three 'arrows' to try to get a 'bullseye'.

Explain that the most common definition of sin in the Bible is that of 'missing the mark' (bullseye); not living up to the perfect laws of God; falling short of them (Rom. 3:23).

As an alternative way of closing . . .

Read together (or in small groups) the whole of Romans 6. Then offer each person a number of pieces of paper and a pen. Ask them to write down the areas of sin that they are having most difficulties with at this time. Taking the emphasis from the passage about burial, have a ceremonial sin-burying by digging a hole (in the garden) and dropping the individual pieces of paper into it.

Close with a prayer of commitment declaring that those sins have been buried with Christ by his death on the cross.

12

Guilt (1)

I'M FEELING GUILTY BECAUSE I'VE FAILED TO KEEP IN TOUCH WITH MY FRIEND JOHN IN SPAIN

I DIDN'T PRAY OR READ MY BIBLE TODAY, AND GOD KNOWS HOW GUILTY I FEEL

I'M FEELING GUILTY BECAUSE I GAVE SOMEONE TOO MUCH LIP AND BECAUSE I FAILED THAT BIG EXAM

I HAVE A GUILT COMPLEX BECAUSE I DON'T GIVE MY PARENTS THE TIME I SHOULD

GUILT DRIVES ME MAD, SCREWS UP MY INSIDES AND IS TEARING ME APART

You can add a lot more comments about guilt. It is one of the few emotions that we rarely get to grips with.

Why? Because to get rid of it, we need to bare our soul to someone . . . and that someone is God.

Let's get into 'guilt' in a big way, in order to be shot of it.

Group instructions

Pass out paper and pens and ask your group to react anonymously on paper to the word 'guilt' – not just what it means, but what it means to them. No long sentences are necessary, but words they may associate with guilt.

Give them just a couple of minutes and then have the papers returned. Read out what is on the sheets and arrange for a summary phrase or word for each one, to be written out on a board, flipchart or overhead projector. Make no comments as you do this.

Split your group into fours and give each group a card with one of the situations listed below.

Give them 20 minutes to think, plan and practise a playlet asking

them to give special thought to the way guilt affects the way we react; not only in our speech but also in the way it changes our facial features and body posture.

The playlet is to last no more than 3 minutes. Adapt the situations if they are not felt to be appropriate.

Situation 1

Tom (17) takes £20 from his mum's purse hoping to return it within a couple of days before she notices. Tom is found out, and after a flaming row, Mum decides to tell Dad.

Tom is in bed when Dad arrives home after his night shift. Mum tells Dad. Dad blows his top, but decides to try and play it cool.

Tom comes down to breakfast knowing that everyone, including his sister, knows . . .

Take it from there.

Situation 2

Mary (15), a good worker at school, and someone who gets on well with her teachers, is persuaded by her friends to go for a smoke during break.

'Snoddles', one of the senior teachers, catches Mary and her friends behind the bike shed smoking.

They are standing outside the Head's study and she feels very guilty.

They are to enter one by one . . .

Take it from outside the Head's room, to include Mary's interview inside.

Situation 3

You lied to your best friend. You've never done it before, but you had gone out with her boyfriend the night before without her knowing.

Take it from the point when you are out with him and tell him that you feel really guilty. Then change the scene to the next day when your best friend confronts you . . . and she knows!

Situation 4

You fail to turn up to give your 'testimony' at church on Sunday evening. You had decided, instead, to go to a rock concert in the city.

Next week you meet the minister at the church door . . .

Take it from there.

● Discuss each playlet afterwards, drawing all the major points together about the way guilt affects us and other people as demonstrated in the playlets.

Research

Read together Matthew 18:21-35. Explain that in this session we are going to concentrate on guilt. This is brought on by the fact that we have not received forgiveness from God and because we have failed to forgive others.

Application: Peter had asked Jesus how many times he should forgive someone, and then typically made a suggestion of seven times.

In fact, he had been very generous.

According to rabbinical tradition (Rabbi Jose Ben Hania) you only had to forgive someone three times!

Peter had multiplied by two and added one for luck! Jesus then takes Peter's generosity and multiplies it, to show how endless our forgiveness for others should be.

The contrast between the two debts is in the extreme. The ruler (King) forgave his servant a debt of 10,000 talents. A 'talent' in this text is equivalent to a person's wage for fifteen years. The King's servant would not forgive his own servant a debt of just 100 denarii, yet a 'denarius' would be the payment for one day's labour.

To make a comparison, the servant owed his King £1,000,000 and was let off the debt, yet the servant didn't forgive and forget his own servant's debt of £2.

Forgiving others, then, must never cease and we must take practical steps to forgive others.

Follow on

Ask your group to make a list of all those people who, by their attitude, speech or action, they may have upset. If they genuinely want to know God's forgiveness and experience a greater depth of love, they should go and apologise.

It may be a friend, minister, parent, teacher, youth leader, work colleague or boss. Encourage this action or this session will have no meaning.

Close with the Family/Lord's prayer, giving special emphasis to 'Forgive us our sins/trespasses, as we forgive others'. (From Matthew 6:9-15.)

> "BEAR WITH THE FAULTS AND FRAILTIES OF OTHERS, FOR YOU, TOO, HAVE MANY FAULTS WHICH OTHERS HAVE TO BEAR. IF YOU CANNOT MOULD YOURSELF AS YOU WOULD WISH, HOW CAN YOU EXPECT OTHER PEOPLE TO BE ENTIRELY TO YOUR LIKING?" – THOMAS À KEMPIS.

13

Guilt (2)

We're looking at guilt again. You may find it helpful to have a gap between this and the previous outline, as guilt can be an emotive and highly-charged subject.

The previous outline dealt with guilt as a result primarily of our wrong relationships with other people. This time we'll be looking at how we recognise guilt and how we can dispose of it.

Don't pass over some of the exercises simply because of *your own* anxiety. The result of the exercises may be very precious for some people, even though they may be painful.

Preparation

Arrange for a couple of your more extrovert characters to act out the parts of a psychiatrist and a patient. The psychiatrist should sit on a chair with a clipboard. If possible arrange for the psychiatrist to wear a white coat. Have a tape recorder set up on a low table.

Make the 'patient' lie down on the table (provide a pillow) in a relaxed position ready for 'the consultation'.

Your chosen psychiatrist should prepare a number of personal, leading questions and the patient should make up answers which reveal the course of his or her past life. For obvious reasons you must look at the proposed scripts beforehand and make sure they are semi-humorous.

On the night

With all your props ready, start the evening with the above sketch. It shouldn't last for more than seven minutes.

Explain that a lot of modern psychiatry is in the business of bringing people's past out into the open – the things they have done, how they feel about themselves and what they feel about other people.

But what do we do with guilt, resentment and jealousy which has built up over the years?

Is it good enough just to bring things into the open? The answer is obviously 'NO' because it is essential to be *released* from guilt, to be able to offer forgiveness to others, and to mend broken relationships via reconciliation. Failure to dispose of one's guilt leads to a life that is ridden with anxiety and fear.

Discussion

Ask the group to discuss with you the various signs of guilt that they have noticed in themselves, their parents and others. Attempt to produce a descriptive list like this from their comments:

- **Depression:** Continual moodiness punctuated by feelings of hopelessness and worthlessness.
- **Aggression:** Tendency to react negatively to those who have the same failings you have noticed in yourself.
- **Apathy and indifference:** As feelings are suppressed and stifled, so the body tends gradually to close down.
- **Anger:** Striking out at others because you feel trapped by blame.
- **Perfectionism:** Occurs because

you feel so guilty you try to create an ideal world for yourself and become a perfectionist in what you are doing.

● **Self-degradation:** Continually turning your guilt feelings inward hoping that when you make a negative comment about yourself someone will contradict you, thus taking the pressure off a bit.

Mention briefly that there is a distinction between what is 'real' guilt and what is false guilt. Explain that often people confuse guilt which arises from breaking social taboos (prohibitions), with that which arises from breaking God's laws and these may not necessarily be the same. Ask for any examples that come to mind but don't make a big thing of them.

Action
Pass out a workcard or sheet for each person entitled 'Forgiveness' and give them 12 minutes to complete it by themselves. Explain that no one will see the card:

Explain that forgiveness from sin and guilt does not come cheaply. We must:

● **Recognise our 'sin',** and call it 'sin' (rebellion against God) and make no excuses for it, as excuses won't hold water with God.

● **Recognise that Jesus died for our sin.** Christ, the Son of God, died that I could be free from guilt. That was no small thing. Read 1 Corinthians 6:19-20. Try to picture Christ dying for the one sin you mentioned on your worksheet/card.

● **Ask God to forgive us and clean us up.** Ask God for his strength so that you don't do it again. (Read Phil. 4:13.)

Forgiveness
1. What failure/sin do I have that I now feel guilty about? (Just the one that is foremost in your mind.)
2. What makes that one more important than all the others? What effect does it have on me?
3. How do I think that God feels about that, right now?
4. What difference do I think 1 John 1:7-10 and 2:2 make to me in the light of what I have said above?

STRICTLY PRIVATE

● **Then forget it.** Jeremiah 31:34 says '... I will forgive their sins and I will no longer remember their wrongs. I, the Lord, have spoken'.
   Isaiah 44:21-22 '... I created you to be my servant, and I will never forget you. I have swept your sins away like a cloud. Come back to me; I am the one who saves you.' (GNB)
   The devil tries to tell us that we haven't really been forgiven, that we should still feel 'up-tight'. But God has said he remembers our sin no more – so why should we?

Letter time
Provide your group with paper and an envelope and ask them to write a letter to God explaining the way they feel and asking for forgiveness.
   The letters should start: 'Dear God, I am so sorry for ...'
   They should take the letters away with them, to keep or destroy as they decide.

Warning
As this session contains a strong element of emotion (no excuses) you should not play on this, so quietly and confidently finish with some prayers of thanksgiving.

14

Competition

From your first cry to your dying breath you are called upon to be competitive – in exams, looks, fashion, even in the car and house you choose. In the words of Vince Lombardi, 'Winning isn't everything; it's the only thing.'

This outline looks at competition. Or, to sum it up, 'when I stand on you, I look taller.'

Preparation

Let's be stupid. Have available some old newspapers. Arrange for one of your group to demonstrate to the others how to make paper aeroplanes with sheets of newspaper.

Place a waste-paper bin at a suitable distance from a marker, and arrange for each of your group (in turn) to attempt to throw their aeroplanes into the bin.

Those who are successful should then have a 'play off' to decide the winner. I suggest you ask them to put their names on each aeroplane so there are no arguments.

Discussion questions

for the groups, to last no more than 22 minutes.
1. Do you think that competition increases or decreases your effectiveness? Why?
2. When and how is competition a negative influence? Please give examples.
3. Why do people feel 'good' once they have won?

4. Have you ever felt 'hurt' when you have lost or failed at something? When and why?
5. Do you like competing? If so, please give reasons.
6. What is your definition of 'winning' and 'losing'?
7. If you had a choice would you live in a society that was with or without competition? Reasons please.

> Split your group into study units of two or three people and ask them to complete the 'Competition Questionnaire' below. You will need one copy per group.

Competition Questionnaire

Read each passage carefully. Tick the appropriate side of 'Positive/Negative', according to whether you feel that the competitive situation was healthy or otherwise. Give your reasons under the heading 'Comments'. You will need to define the competitive element in the passage first (sometimes it is only implied).

Passage	Positive/Negative	Comments
Luke 4:1-14		
Mark 14:32-42		
Philippians 3:12-14		
Genesis 37:2-11		
Job 1:6-12		

What Jesus thought

Jesus' idea of competitiveness and winning is very different from that put forward by our society today. For Jesus, winning was not being number one, but instead doing the will of his Father.

Jesus' dying on the cross was a victory – he won. Yet it was a far cry from being number one and powerful.

To win, then, as a Christian, is to serve. It is only our deceptive nature that sees winning as being better or being more powerful than someone else. That does not mean that we shouldn't be ambitious and competitive. It is our motive and goals that are important.

Follow on

Ask your group to be practical and write down what areas of their life they're going to change in light of their discussion. Do this in the following way:

Write on a board or overhead projector, or read slowly, a number of subjects. Your group should write them down and note down their changes anonymously.

SUGGESTIONS: school, work, parents, brothers and sisters, church, sports, appearance, leadership, opposite sex, exams, possessions. Add any more as appropriate.

Finally, with the thoughts still uppermost in their minds of how they will change their attitude/behaviour in these areas, read a small passage from *The Hobbit* by J R R Tolkien:

'Good-bye!' said Gandalf to Thorin. 'And good-bye to you all, good-bye! Straight through the forest is your way now. Don't stray off the track! – If you do, it is a thousand to one you will never find it again, and never get out of Mirkwood, and then I don't suppose I, or any one else, will ever see you again'.

'Do we really have to go through?' groaned the Hobbit.

'Yes, you do!' said the Wizard, 'If you want to get to the other side. You must go through or give up your quest. And I am not going to allow you to back out now, Mr. Baggins. I am ashamed of you for thinking of it'.

15

Judgementalism

It was the learned rabbis who taught that there were six great works that each Jew should attempt to perform.

Those six were: study, visiting the sick, hospitality, devotion in prayer, education of children in God's law and thinking the best of other people.

The latter 'work' is largely a neglected trait of the western Christian. Negative criticism of each other as Christians has been one of the most effective tools of the devil today – from the odd remark about the vicar's wife to the behaviour of the young people. It seems a far cry from Jesus' remarks to his disciples – 'Do not judge others, so that God will not judge you.' (Matt. 7:1, GNB.)

Action

As your group arrives make a point of criticising their dress, their comments and their behaviour. Make sure you do this in an overt way. Criticise the last Sunday service, the weather, coffee, etc. Whatever you say, be completely negative.

Read

Most of you found that when you did the test the young man didn't come out too well. In fact, most of us tend to think the worst of other people and are not slow, therefore, in criticising them. Ask the group to read with you 'the' passage on the subject (Matt. 7:1-5). Jesus is not against objective judgement made in a clear and impartial manner but against censoriousness (fault-finding) for the sake of it.

Ask each group member to write down the names of three people whom they have recently criticised. This must be done (obviously)

Test

Arrange for the following grammar test to be duplicated for each member of the group. Allow five minutes for them to complete this test.

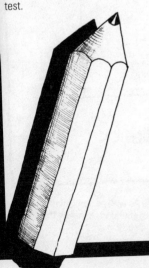

Grammar

Mark this paragraph into sentences. Use capitals, full stops and commas etc., where needed:

'He is a young man yet experienced in vice and wickedness he is never found in opposing the works of iniquity he takes delight in the downfall of his neighbours he never rejoices in the prosperity of his fellow-creatures he is always ready to assist in destroying the peace of society he takes no pleasure in serving the Lord he is uncommonly diligent in sowing discord among his friends and acquaintances he takes no pride in labouring to promote the cause of Christianity he has not been negligent in endeavouring to tear down the church he makes no effort to subdue his evil passions he strives hard to build up Satan's kingdom he lends no aid to the support of the gospel among the heathen he contributes largely to the devil he will never go to heaven he must go where he will receive his just reward'.
(Ron Main)

Pass out the corrected sheet for comparison.

Grammar test – correct answer

'He is a young man, yet experienced. In vice and wickedness, he is never found. In opposing the works of iniquity, he takes delight. In the downfall of his neighbours, he never rejoices. In the prosperity of his fellow creatures, he is always ready to assist. In destroying the peace of society, he takes no pleasure. In serving the Lord, he is uncommonly diligent. In sowing discord among his friends and acquaintances, he takes no pride. In labouring to promote the cause of Christianity, he has not been negligent. In endeavouring to tear down the church, he makes no effort. To subdue his evil passions, he strives hard. To build up Satan's kingdom, he lends no aid. To the support of the gospel among the heathen, he contributes largely. To the Devil he will never go. To Heaven he must go, where he will receive his just reward'.

privately. Against each name they are to write a few words of criticism that they have thought or expressed.

Ask your group what is actually being said about our own faults in verses four and five.

We often see faults in ourselves that we exaggerate in others, so minimising the gravity of our own, and transferring the attention away from ourselves. Instead of repenting over our own faults we take pleasure in self-righteousness. This is the picture in the classic story Jesus told in Luke 18:9-14 (the Pharisee and the sinner).

A speck in the eye is very irritating and uncomfortable. We call it a foreign body. Our responsibility as Christians is to take out the log from our own eye, before having the presumption and audacity to try and remove the speck of dust from someone else's!

Suggest three reasons why no one can judge another person:

1. We never know all the facts, or the whole person.
2. It is almost impossible for any one to be strictly impartial in his or her judgement.
3. No one is good enough to judge anyone else.

Summarise by reading a quotation from John Stott on this subject: 'The command to "judge not" is not a requirement to be blind, but rather a plea to be generous. Jesus does not tell us to cease to be men (by suspending our critical powers which help to distinguish us from animals) but to renounce the presumptuous ambition to be God (by setting ourselves up as judges)'. (From 'Christian Counter-culture'.)

Demonstration

To demonstrate the absolute foolishness of such fault-finding in others, set up and attempt Matthew 7:4,5. As well as being humorous, as Jesus intended, it makes the point very clearly.

WHAT ABOUT...?

16 *Prayer*

How should we pray? When difficult situations face us, how should we petition God?

Of course, it's not just when we've got problems that we need to pray.

This session homes in on the question 'How should we pray?' – and discovers what Jesus said.

Prayer is often bound up with ecclesiastical jargon and meaningless clichés like 'a word of prayer', and 'let us pray for the whole world'.

Ask your group to list some of the jargon and the many prayer clichés that exist.

Discuss

After spending no more than 4 minutes doing this, ask 'What do jargon and clichés normally cover up?'

Discover

So how should we pray? This is a question that the disciples asked Jesus. (See Luke 11:1-4 and Matt. 6:9-15.)

I have often maintained that what we call 'The Lord's Prayer' or 'The Family Prayer' would be better titled 'The Disciples' Prayer'. It can only be truly prayed by a disciple of Jesus to have any real meaning and relevance.

Look together at the Matthew passage (6:9-15):
● The first three petitions are all to do with **God's glory:** 'May your holy name be honoured; may your kingdom come; may your will be done on earth as it is in heaven'.
● The second three speak in turn of **the present, past and future.** All these contain needs that we want God to attend to:

'Give us today the food we need. Forgive us the wrongs we have done, as we forgive the wrongs that others have done to us. Do not bring us to hard testing'.

This prayer becomes more astonishing as you digest it. It even presupposes the Trinity: we are asking God the Father to sustain us, for forgiveness through Jesus Christ, and, for the future, the help of the Holy Spirit to be our comforter, guide, strength and illuminator.

It is clear that prayer for self must be expressed out of an attitude of praise to God.

Action

Spread out a large pile of magazines and newspapers on the floor and ask each person to tear out an article or picture that expresses:
● something of the mighty and powerful creation of God;
● the request for our daily provision to maintain life;
● forgiveness;
● the future and our involvement in it.

Each person should now have four items.

Meditation

Ask the group to take each of their items (starting with the first listed) and look at it. Suggest that they ask God to help them know what to say to him now, quietly, in prayer. Read from Psalm 46, 'Be still, and know that I am God'. Then allow a few minutes for silent prayer.

Encourage your group to read a psalm a day and quietly meditate upon it.

For the Jew of the Bible, prayer and life were intrinsically caught up with each other. Every Jew (ideally) prayed three times a day (Ps. 55:17, Dan. 6:10). There were family prayers at the beginning and end of the sabbath, as well as before and after every meat dish.

Those of you old enough to remember the film 'Fiddler on the Roof' will remember the constant life of prayer and petition of the main character. If you can, obtain the soundtrack of the film and play a couple of songs. 'The Sabbath song' is a good example.

16

Read

Jesus promises to answer prayer. Read Luke 11:9-13 where we find the key words:

Ask and you *will* receive
Seek and you *will* find
Knock and the door *will* be opened to you

The key is in the first letter of each of the first words – **ASK**. We need to come to terms with the fact that, at its simplest, prayer answers are often like traffic lights: 'No', 'Wait', and 'Yes'. At its most complicated it's like the colours of the rainbow where the colours merge into one another.

Sadly, we very often pray vaguely and therefore become vague in our expectations. We then become frustrated and may secretly think that God doesn't really answer prayer.

I leave you with this thought:

No prayers: No answers
Vague prayers: Vague answers
Specific prayers: Specific answers

Remember that even silence may be an answer.

'WHEN YOU PRAY, DO NOT HEAP UP EMPTY PHRASES.'

Matt 6:7

17 The uniqueness of Christ

Why Jesus? Why not Buddha? Why not Muhammad?

What's so special about Christianity? We all follow the same God anyway, don't we?

With the march of Islamic fundamentalism, the 'jihad' (holy war) and the evangelistic zeal which has arisen in the Islamic world, should we be concerned at all? Muslims worship Allah, the one true God, so what is the problem?

Activities

Begin by reading this prayer. Don't say where it's from.

Praise be to God, the Lord of the worlds! The compassionate, the merciful! King of the day of judgement! Thee only do we worship and to thee do we cry for help. Guide Thou us on the straight path, the path of those to whom Thou has been gracious – with whom Thou art not angry and who go not astray.

This, in fact, is the most common prayer among the Muslims, the words of Sura 1 of the Qur'an.

● **Association of thought.** Ask the group to write down any words, phrases and comments which come to mind when they hear the expression, Islamic faith. Help them by adding other words, e.g. Muhammad, Mecca, prayer mat, etc.

As your group express their offerings it will give you and the others an idea of how much (or how little) they know.

Be warned. They may know more than you. Many schools have for many years been teaching comparative religions and they may well be conversant with different religious beliefs.

● Split your group into units of four or five and ask them to make up their own religion. Give them twenty minutes and use the questions in the box to help.

● Serious feedback is essential and you should allow time to hear your group's views. This exercise should be meaningful in itself and not just a springboard for the major points you are to look at later. Therefore take real interest as it will also show their real feelings and doubts about God!

● With your group together, and after very clear preparation by looking at the Bible verses offered, make a comparison of Islam with Christianity.

17

Comparison

ISLAM	CHRISTIANITY
1. Islam is a religion of the book: The Qur'an.	**1.** Christianity is a religion of the book: The Bible.
2. Muslims worship Allah who is a god outside and beyond our lives.	**2.** God for the Christian is someone . . . (Luke 15:11-32).
3. Islam converts are enrolled on the confession of the creed: 'There is no deity but Allah and Muhammad is the prophet of God'.	**3.** Christianity claims that Jesus is . . . and that God is . . . (Colossians 1:15-20).
4. In Islamic teaching, Allah's creatures cannot affect him for he is wholly independent and has preordained all things, e.g., if someone falls under a lorry Muslims would say, 'The will of Allah!'	**4.** Christianity professes a God who is vitally concerned with his creatures (1 John 4:7-10, John 3:16).
5. The follower must submit to the will of Allah. 'Islam' means 'submission'.	**5.** Christians are called to obey their father (John 15:10).
6. Islam does not promise communion with God in worship, for worship is simply a service which Allah has commanded.	**6.** Christians' belief is very different when it comes to worship. Why? (Ephesians 2:18).
7. Islam claims that Jesus didn't die, only someone like Jesus, Sura IV.	**7.** Christianity believes in Jesus as God dying publicly on a cross (Mark 15:33-41).

Summary

Islam is a very mechanical faith. God is seen to be 'out there' and not involved with his creatures or creation. One Islamic theologian in the 12th century was executed for saying that God was as close to him as 'the vein on his neck'.

In Islamic faith there is no place for a personal, compassionate God. Heaven is the place you go to if you have done more good deeds than bad.

Christianity is about a relationship with a person – Jesus, the Son of God – who in a loving and caring relationship chooses to involve himself with people, even to allow his own death on the cross.

Our place is not to condemn but to pray for, and to seek to love, those who reject Christ, because they, too, need the closeness of Jesus.

● **Highly recommended:** The Lion Handbook of World Religions (*Lion;* £9.95).

Make up your own religion

1. What is the god (if any) of your religion like?
2. What demands does he/she make on you? How does the god act and how are you expected to act?
3. How do you worship and pray?
4. What is your code of practice, i.e. who is in charge? Who checks that you are doing things properly?
5. How is your religion financed?
6. Where do you meet?
7. Do you spread your religion? If so how?
8. Do you have a book to follow?
9. What happens to those who don't want to follow your religion?
10. What things make your religion so special?

18 *Reliability of the Gospels*

With a conspiratorial move of the head our friend leans closer and delivers the titbit.

'Simon and Jane were at the party you know. They've been seeing a lot of each other recently.'

Our response when it comes, is a subtle mixture of shock at Simon and Jane's supposed indescretion, and delight that we're 'in the know.'

'And Jane's married!'

You and I are only too aware of the process whereby something very innocent is seen or heard; but, by the time the rumour has passed between a few people, it has become distorted and is far from the truth.

Watching a recent Channel 4 TV series on 'The First Christians' I was appalled at the sweeping statements which implied that the Gospel writers got things confused.

Similarly, London Weekend Television's 'Jesus: The Evidence' offered wild conjecture as plain fact. So a very important subject to look at is the relationship of truth to the Jesus of the Bible. Pilate's question to Jesus, a question that is now famous, was 'What is truth?' Sadly, Pilate didn't wait for an answer!

Action

Ask for a coin – preferably a 10p or 50p piece. Place it in your fingers, as if you were going to flick it.

Ask one or two people from different parts of the room to confirm that the coin is showing 'heads'.

With everyone watching, flick the coin in the air and let it land on the floor. Ask two or three people to leave their seats to confirm what side of the coin is showing.

Then pick up the coin and return it to the lender. Make a few cracks about there being no interest etc . . . Give each person a blank piece of

paper and ask them to put their name and the date on the top. Give them 7 minutes to write a fifty-word commentary on exactly what happened from the moment you asked for the coin until you returned the same.

Take in the reports and read each one. If you have a very large group – twenty or more – shuffle them and read no more than fifteen.

Assuming that no-one has deliberately lied, make the following comments about their accounts:

1. They're all written in different styles.
2. They all claim to be true.
3. They all offer different facts.
4. They all display varying degrees of literary skills.
5. They were all written by eye-witnesses.

Read to the group the following: 'The four Gospels give eye-witness accounts of the life, death and resurrection of Jesus. But they are far from being word-for-word the same, although it appears that both

Show from this chart that we have very many manuscripts of the Gospels, compared with the numbers of other 'acceptable' historical documents. It is important that the group studies this chart carefully, so you may need to draw up a large version of it.

Matthew and Luke used a considerable amount of Mark in their accounts.

All of them appear to have their different sources – and together they help to create a picture of the life and teachings of Jesus, which we call "gospel truth".

Go over points 1 to 4 again, relating them to the Gospels. For 5, point out that the Gospels were all written on the basis of checked accounts of eye-witnesses. For example, according to Papias – one of the early 'Christian Fathers' – it seems that Peter was behind Mark's Gospel, Peter relating to Mark what he had seen and heard.

Split your group into four and give each group a card with one of the following passages on it:
● Matthew 28:1-10; ● Mark 16:1-10; ● Luke 24:1-12; ● John 20:1-10.

Ask each group to pull out the salient features from the passage to include:
● The sequence of events
● The people involved
● The places and objects mentioned

18

Give them 20 minutes to do this, and then put the Mark and Matthew, and Luke and John groups together to discuss the similarities and differences.

Read again '1-5' and help them understand that 'differences' don't need to be a problem – on the contrary, the differences in the Gospels enhance the story they put together.

In the final analysis we cannot prove the resurrection to anybody. As John Stott says, 'Perhaps the transformation of the disciples of Jesus is the greatest evidence of all for the resurrection.'

Give each person a pen and a piece of paper. Ask everyone to write, on one side, a letter to a non-Christian friend. It should tell him/her how the resurrected Jesus has given them a new life and what differences this new life has made.

Ask them to write, on the other

side, a letter to God – thanking him for Jesus and saying what his resurrected life has done for them. If some of your group don't have a Christian commitment explain that, if they wish, they could write asking for

the new life Jesus can bring.

Invite members of your group to read their letters to God and, to finish on a strong Easter note, treat the read-aloud letters as prayers.

Ancient Writing	The History of Thucydides	Caesar's Gallic War	Tacitus' Histories	The Four Gospels
(A) Original documental writers	460-400 BC	58-50 BC	Approx. AD 100	AD 65-90
(B) Oldest surviving copy	AD 900 (plus a few 1st Century fragments)	AD 850	AD 800	AD 350 (even earlier for fragments)
(C) Approx. time between (A) and (B)	1300 years (fragments 400 years)	900 years	700 years	300 years (fragments 50 years)
(D) Number of ancient copies in existence today	8	10	4	up to 2000

19 Fobbing off the Bible

Why don't we believe the Bible? The Bible says, 'Go into all the world and preach the Gospel.' So why do we sit down and ask God whether we have a 'call' to the mission field?

I DIDN'T SEE THAT HAPPEN!

It's the wrong question. We should be asking God whether it is necessary for us to stay.

The Bible records Jesus' words to the rich young ruler as 'sell all that you have and follow me.' Words just for the rich young ruler or for us too? We fob off the Bible for several reasons and this month we're going to look at two of them: (1) The accounts of events in Jesus' lifetime differ, therefore they can't be taken too seriously. (2) The things the Bible says were relevant for that time only and don't necessarily apply to us today.

We have to learn to walk the fine line between getting the Bible in context and fobbing it off altogether.

Activity

Set up an incident with the help of a few friends outside the group and preferably unknown to the group.
Suggestion: Arrange to go on an evening stroll, ramble, crawl, or whatever term you might like to give to your evening. Now you need to use some imagination: arrange for something quite dramatic to happen right in front of your group – a robbery, mugging, fight, crash.

Ideally it should happen when your group are spread out a bit so that they don't all see it from the same distance. Even more fantastic would be for you as the youth leader to become part of it and maybe end up an injured party.

Whatever you do, it will need to be well rehearsed. Some local drama club may love to do this for you. Whatever you do, if it involves something looking criminal you must seek permission of the police.

Hand out paper there and then. Ask them to write an incident report showing exactly what happened. After giving them thirteen minutes to do this, you should have some of them read out their reports.

Discuss with them:
1. Why the accounts are written in different literary styles.
2. Why the reports agree in the main but differ in detail.
3. What difference geographical position makes to the accuracy of the report.
4. What you would need to do to write an accurate account of the incident having the people involved and the witnesses' accounts available.

19

Suggestion: If you had a really clever investigator in your group you could have him interview everyone and then give a summary of what seem to be the facts. Even more impressive would be to find a real detective and have him interview everyone and then give his report.

You need to get across to the group the point that the Bible is reliable. The Gospel accounts are different because they reflect the personalities and literary skills of the writers and their closeness to the information. As a leader you should do some background reading to the gospels or collar your minister for some advice.

Prepare a tray with about twenty-five items on it, e.g: pencil, match, ornament. Arrange for some items to be large so that from certain angles some smaller items are out of view. No moving of positions.

Give everyone thirty seconds to view the tray, remove it from the room and ask each member of your group to write down the items they remember.

Lead a discussion along the lines of:
1. Why did someone remember twenty-two items while another remembered only nine?
2. Why did some remember certain types of items while others did not?
3. What difference did the seating arrangements make to the number of items seen?

4. What light does this discussion throw on the reason for the different Gospel accounts?

Finally, and perhaps most importantly, if the Bible is written accurately what relevance does it have for me? Split the group up into fives and ask them to read a passage of the Bible which you designate from the list.

They should decide what relevance it had for the people then, and what we should do now in light of the words which we read today. Jesus was radical – how radical are we going to be in applying the words of Jesus in our lives?

Each group should give brief feedback. Each person should then write a few lines indicating their 'intention' in light of what they have learnt.

A full programme, but well worth it.

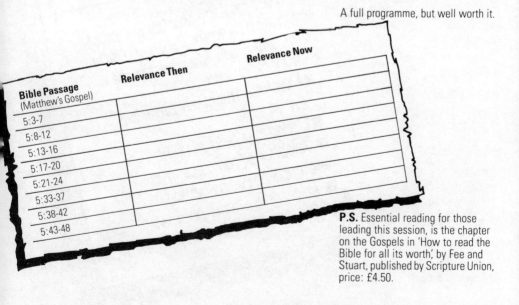

Bible Passage (Matthew's Gospel)	Relevance Then	Relevance Now
5:3-7		
5:8-12		
5:13-16		
5:17-20		
5:21-24		
5:33-37		
5:38-42		
5:43-48		

P.S. Essential reading for those leading this session, is the chapter on the Gospels in 'How to read the Bible for all its worth', by Fee and Stuart, published by Scripture Union, price: £4.50.

20  *Meditation*

JESUS: THE WAY, THE TRUTH, THE LIFE

Meditation is often passed over in preference to the louder, more exuberant time of group worship, but there is a place for both.

Thomas, one of Jesus' more earnest and honest disciples said '. . . how can we know the way?' (John 14:5). Jesus never side-stepped the genuine enquirer. He put the answer very bluntly: 'I am the WAY and the TRUTH and the LIFE. No-one comes to the Father except through me.'

JESUS SAID, 'I AM THE WAY'

Get hold of some Ordnance Survey maps, enough for one map between four or five people. The library should be able to help you. The maps do not need to be the same. On each map, paperclip the following instructions:

You are to give instructions for a group of people who are travelling on a 3-day hike from _____ to _____ *

You must find the shortest but most reasonable route for the group using paths and roads. You must make allowances for them to:

■ Purchase their daily provisions EN ROUTE.

■ Camp in a field at night.

■ Telephone from near their campsite each evening.

■ Take some scenic photos.

All directions are to be carefully written.

*As the leader you fill in the places which you have decided upon.

Action

As your group arrive, have lots of holiday brochures lying around to give an atmosphere of travel. Give them time to browse through the brochures before you officially start.

Split them into groups of four or five and give them their assignments. Give them 15 minutes to complete the exercise.

After 15 minutes, whether they have finished or not, ask a representative from each group to read out some of the directions.

Meditation

Jesus said 'I am the WAY'. Jesus is not someone who just gives us directions and shows us the way, he actually travels with us to show us the way – he becomes the 'WAY' for us. Across the difficult terrain of our lives, he doesn't watch from a distance but travels alongside us. When we are not sure which way to go, he is there at that point guiding us.

As the leader, quietly echo similar words to the above, but leave pauses so that the group have a chance to think them through.

JESUS SAID, 'I AM THE TRUTH'

Give them four minutes to complete the true/false questionnaire and then give the answers . . .

20

Meditation

Jesus said 'I am the TRUTH'. There are many people who say that they know the truth. There are many who say, 'I have taught the truth', but it is only Jesus who says 'I am the truth'. Jesus will never lie to you or try to trick you. When you are facing decisions of whether to tell the truth or to lie to others, he will help you make the right decision and help you to face the consequences.

JESUS SAID, 'I AM THE LIFE'

Action

Get everybody to stand up and ask them to run on the spot for one minute as fast as they can. Give them other strenuous exercises that you as the leader can cope with!

Meditation

Jesus said, 'I am the LIFE'. Every breath we breathe is given to us by God. Jesus says, 'I have come in order that you might have life – life in all its fullness' (John 10:10, GNB). To fall in love with Christ is to fall in love with life. Our very being exists to show the purposes of God. Jesus said, 'I am the WAY and the TRUTH and the LIFE. No one comes to the Father except through me.'

NB: as the leader you should prepare the meeting very carefully to provide continuity and an atmosphere of reverence.

Action

True or false?

1. Mary gave birth to Jesus in Nazareth.

2. Light travels at approximately 186,000 miles per second.

3. Jesus was 100 per cent God and 100 per cent man.

4. Moses took two of every creature into the ark with him.

5. Matthew and Mark are the only two Gospels to give the account of Jesus' birth.

6. After our 'first' teeth fall out we grow 36 teeth.

7. We see upside down. Our brain makes the adjustment.

8. It was Abraham who attempted to sacrifice Isaac.

9. A 'trachea' is another word for windpipe.

10. Abel killed Cain.

	TRUE	FALSE
1	☐	☐
2	☐	☐
3	☐	☐
4	☐	☐
5	☐	☐
6	☐	☐
7	☐	☐
8	☐	☐
9	☐	☐
10	☐	☐

Answers: 1. False. It was Bethlehem. 2. True. 3. True. 4. False. It was Noah. 5. False. It is Matthew and Luke. 6. False. We have 32 teeth. 7. True. 8. True. 9. True. 10. False. Cain killed Abel.

21

Sex is a drive and we need someone at the wheel.
    One look at the agony columns in women's magazines shows that many young people are dealing with a runaway truck!

Sometimes you can't believe what you read. One letter I found recently went something like this:

A guy had written to the agony aunt about two girls he was dating and having sex with. They both found out about each other and broke off their relationship with the guy. He wanted to know what to do and ended his letter with, 'Do not give me any more of this morality jazz, but help'. He signed it, 'Discouraged'.
    The agony columnist's response was brilliant. 'Dear Discouraged, the basic difference between man and animals is morality, and if you don't want any then I suggest you go to see a vet'.
    God made sex to be enjoyed within a loving, caring relationship of marriage.

What is love?
Pass out a piece of paper and a pen to each person with the words:

● LOVE IS . . . Give them four minutes to jot down what comes into their heads. Then ask them to turn over the sheet:
● LOVE IS NOT . . . and again give them four minutes to complete their list.
● Then, on a large sheet of paper, make a list of all the 'love is' and 'love is nots'.

Action
Split your group into four units and ask two of the units to produce a three-minute sketch on what 'love is' on a date and the other two what

'love is not' on a date. I would strongly recommend, for obvious reasons, that the emphasis should be on verbal communication between the actors and actresses.

Research

Together, look at 1 Corinthians 13:4-7.

Give each person another piece of paper and ask them to list, in one column, what the Bible says love is.

Go through the biblical list and then ask them to add, individually, a few words in the second column on what this means to a relationship, now or in the future, with a member of the opposite sex.

Love is...

Bible	For my relationship it means ...
Patient	eg. I will try to listen more.
Kind	eg. I will think more about what he wants to do.
Not boastful	
Not proud	
Not rude	
Not selfish	
Not irritable	
Does not keep records of wrongs	
Not happy with evil	
Truthful	
Not for giving up	

Explain

How far should you go on a date? Explain the following in your own words:

The sex drive is progressive. The first time you hold hands with her – wow! – the sudden exhilaration of that moment. But that does not satisfy and therefore you progress – or regress, depending on your view.

It perhaps could be seen like a graph of time against intensity.

God does not give us 'Ten Commandments of how far you should go on a date'.

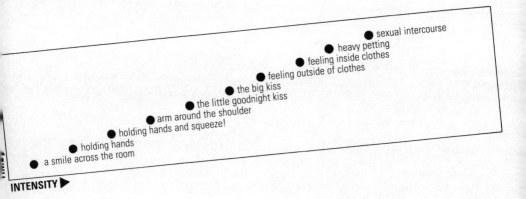

sexual intercourse

heavy petting

feeling inside clothes

feeling outside of clothes

the big kiss

the little goodnight kiss

arm around the shoulder

holding hands and squeeze!

holding hands

a smile across the room

INTENSITY ▶

If he did we would all dangle on the extreme, waiting to go on to the next stage. This would lead to intolerable frustration for both parties. God has set his limit on no sexual intercourse outside of marriage.

However, that does not mean we sit on the limit, petting to the extent that we achieve a 'climax' without having intercourse and then state that we are technically still virgins.

God is more interested in the *whole* intimacy of two people who come to terms with the limits before them and take a realistic appraisal together of what a deep caring relationship means.

This will probably mean that you set very clear limits as to the extent of your physical contact. Sex needs someone in control and God can and will help you to be realistic.

For further study on how far you should go on a date: ● Proverbs 6:27-28; ● 1 Thessalonians 4:3-5; ● 2 Timothy 2:22 and ● 1 Peter 2:11.

Important

Give each person some writing paper, pen and an envelope and ask them to address their envelope and letter to God. Their letter should tell God what kind of person they would like to marry and how they would like to see their relationship develop. Ask them to be very honest in what they are asking for. Then they should put the letter in the envelope to be kept for a time when they need to open it.

My acknowledgements to the book 'Dating and Waiting' by Les John Christie.

WHO, ME?!

22

Missionaries

The slide projector stopped abruptly but the general mumble of discontent continued.

After what seemed like 20,000 slides with 20,000 detailed explanations, we looked at our watches to discover that only one hour had elapsed. The rather round, red-faced lady stood up and continued. She looked as if she had just walked out of the 1950s and had fought her way through a jungle of brambles to get here. But then she was a missionary and you expect that kind of thing from them.

Missionary work takes very low priority in most churches. The only profile they ever really get is when the church decides how much to cough up this year, or when the missionary turns up at the church on furlough. (I always used to think that this was something to do with digging up a field!)

Missionaries get the 'dog-ends' of our time, concern, prayer and money. For every six women on the mission field there is only one man. A deplorable situation, yes; but things become absolutely farcical when you consider that men don't allow such missionary women (generally) to play their full role in their local church when they return, even though they have preached and taught on the mission field!

Activity
Begin by passing out this questionnaire to the group. Treat it light-heartedly but make sure they all do it by themselves. You may find that they take it seriously – depending on their preconceptions of 'missionaries'.

Pass out some poster paper and felt-tip pens and, with your group split into smaller units, ask them to draw a picture of their idea of a typical missionary. Again this is to get their preconceptions out of their system.

Questionnaire

To be a Missionary:	TRUE	FALSE
You need to be spiritual	☐	☐
You have to like spiders	☐	☐
You must speak other languages	☐	☐
You can be an office clerk or mechanic	☐	☐
You must not get married	☐	☐
You must hate leaving Britain	☐	☐
You must be able to show slides	☐	☐
You must be able to speak publicly	☐	☐
You must be a bit of a loner	☐	☐
You must live on very little	☐	☐
You don't have temptations and feelings like you and me	☐	☐

Discussion

In small groups, discuss all the following questions and then devise a simple dramatic presentation (2 mins) to demonstrate one answer:

1. What do you think are the most important qualities for a missionary to have and why? (For example: a sense of humour, good language ability, confidence in their faith, etc.)

2. 'You can't be a missionary overseas if you haven't been a missionary in your own home'. Do you agree? Why, or why not?

3. 'Young people are too inexperienced and older people are too inflexible!' What is a good age for working overseas, and why?

4. Do the children of missionaries suffer? What do you think they miss out on and what do you think they gain?

5. 'If you're only there for a year, you've barely begun to understand the people or the language. Short-term work isn't worth much!' What are the 'pros and cons' of short-term and long-term service?

6. 'Missionary work today is about health projects, helping the poor etc., not preaching the gospel!!' Discuss.

Allow time for adequate discussion and preparation (31 mins) and then allow enough time for feedback and presentations (15 mins).

IMPORTANT Write to, or telephone, different missionary organisations and ask for literature about them. Exhibit all interesting materials – particularly on job opportunities.
   Give the group the following sheet, titled 'Attitudes', to work through by themselves at home.

Attitudes

The following are asked to help you check your attitude towards missions:

1. I thank God that I have become a Christian through the Lord Jesus (Rom. 6:23).
2. My career and future is my own business (2 Cor. 5:15).
3. I believe that God has a definite purpose for my life and that this includes witnessing for him somewhere (Eph. 2:10 and Acts 1:8).
4. I believe it is God's will that everybody becomes a Christian, and that includes every nationality (1 Tim. 2:4).
5. I believe that there are many ways to become a Christian apart from through Jesus Christ (Acts 4:12)
6. I would like to work as a missionary but my family responsibilities mean I must stay at home (Mark 10:29-30).
7. My talents would be wasted if I went overseas (Matt. 26:8,9).
8. I'd like to be a missionary but I must have financial security for the future (Matt. 6:33,34).
9. When I read Christ's invitation to 'come', I did, but when I read his command to 'go', I must wait for a special feeling before doing anything about it (Matt. 28:19).
10. I know that there are still millions of people who have no part of the Bible in their own language; whereas more than 90 per cent of all ministers of the gospel are working amongst English speakers (Ezek. 3:18).
11. I believe it is more important that a few hear the gospel many times, than that all hear it once (Rom. 15:20).
12. I realise that the non-Christian religions, the communists and the heretical sects are sending out hundreds of missionaries every year to capture the peoples of the world (2 John:7).
13. In view of all these facts I intend to stay at home, look after myself, and retire in comfort after I have made enough money (Luke 12:20).
14. I humbly declare before God:
a) I am willing to go anywhere for the sake of Jesus, my Lord (Rom. 1:14,15).
b) I am willing to do anything for the sake of Jesus my Lord (Acts 21:13).
c) I am willing to do without anything for the sake of Jesus my Lord (Phil. 3:8).
15. I promise to seek earnestly – by prayer and study – to know God's will for my life (Ezra 8:21).
16. As a first step I will study the needs of one country, and pray for one missionary, write regularly and give to support her/his work (2 Cor. 9:6).

Signed _____ Date _____

Many thanks to Sally Farrant of 'Ruanda Mission' CMS for her assistance.

Fishy business— hooking followers

...sh, fish, fish, and more fish. It was Josephus the famous ...istorian, for a time governor of Galilee, who tells us that in ...is day there were 330 fishing boats which sailed the waters ...f the lake. No wonder the Bible is so full of fishy stories.

So, with a smell all of its own, get hooked into this page ...f ideas and tackle the great fish controversy. No floating ...round on this one – it's sink or swim. (It gets worse!)

...possible, prepare some fish ...elicacies so that the room reeks of ...sh when people arrive.

Read together Mark 1:14-20. Pass ...ut some paper and pens and get ...ur youth group to write a character ...udy of the fishermen that Jesus ...alled to 'follow' him. Give them no ...ore than seven minutes to do this ...nd then choose a few of them to ...ead their studies out.

Read this to the group: ...esus was a man for the people. He ...ands in stark contrast in his attitude ...others. George Bernard Shaw ...aid: "I have never had any feelings ...r the working classes except a ...esire to abolish them and replace ...em with sensible people."

However, a true follower of Jesus ...nnot but love the common man. ...raham Lincoln said: "God must ...ve the common people, he made so ...any of them."

So often we "professionalise" the ...ll of Christ to be "fishers of men" ...calling in the experts to do our job ...r us.

Questions

Ask the group to answer these questions in the light of Mark 1:14-20.
1. Jesus found his 'potentials' fishing. Why did he not choose people for the task who were less busy? What significance has that for us today?
2. What does 'follow me' mean in today's society? Please, no polite platitudes.
3. What was Jesus offering the disciples? CLUE: It was no pearly mansion in the sky.

Take a letter

Passing out some more paper, ask the group to write a reply to Jesus' invitation to 'follow me'. All the letters should start like this: 'Dear Jesus, Thank you for your kind invitation to follow you. I . . .'

On completion of the letters, ask the group to use them as a basis for a silent prayer. They should take them home at the end of the session. The call of Jesus was to become 'fishers of men'. Duplicate, or photocopy the parable below and, after reading it, discuss your thinking and reaction.

A Fishy Parable

'For months, the Fishers' Society had been wracked with dissension. They had built a new meeting hall which they called their Aquarium and had even called a world-renowned Fisherman's Manual scholar to lecture them on the art of fishing. But still no fish were caught.

'Several times each week they would gather in their ornate Aquarium Hall, recite portions of the Fisherman's Manual and then listen to their scholar expound the intricacies and mysteries of the Manual. The meeting would usually end with the scholar dramatically casting his net into the large tank in the centre of the hall and the members rushing excitedly to its edges to see if any fish would bite. None ever did, of course, since there were not any fish in the tank.

'Which brings us to the reason for the controversy. Why? The temperature of the tank was carefully regulated to be just right for ocean perch. Indeed, oceanography experts had been consulted to make the environment of the tank nearly indistinguishable from the ocean. But still no fish. Some blamed it on poor attendance at the society's meetings. Others were convinced that specialisation was the answer: perhaps several small tanks geared especially for different fish age groups.

'There was even division over which was more important: casting, or providing optimum tank conditions.

'Eventually a solution was reached. A few members of the society were commissioned to become professional fishermen and were sent to live a few blocks away on the edge of the sea and do nothing but catch fish.

'It was a lonely existence because most other members of the society were terrified of the ocean. So the professionals would send back pictures of themselves holding some of their catches and letters describing the joys and tribulations of real live fishing.

'And periodically they would return to Aquarium Hall to show slides. After such meetings, people of the society would return to their homes thankful that their hall had not been built in vain.'

(Reprinted from 'The Wittenburg Door'.)

● Finish the evening with a fish and chip supper.

'A nominal Christian'

paused for a moment. 'Of course', I added, 'their Christian faith was only nominal.'

When I realised what I'd said, I felt like kicking myself. Who was I to make sweeping judgements about other people's lives?

It did start me thinking, though, about what it means to be a 'nominal' Christian. Nominality is defined as: 'Existing in name or word only, not actual or real or effective'. Was I one? Are you one? Read on, and you might find out . . .

Pass out sheets of this quick, not really very serious (but do not tell your group that) fun quiz.

CONFIDENTIAL

Are you a nominal Christian?

1. How many times do you:
   ... go to church each week?   1 2 3 4 5 6 7
   ... read your Bible a week?   1 2 3 4 5 6 7
   ... pray each week?   1 2 3 4 5 6 7
   ... witness to friends each week?   1 2 3 4 5 6 7
   ... take communion each week?   1 2 3 4 5 6 7

2. How much money do you give to the church each week?   £1 £5 £10 £25 other

3. How many times are you seen in the pub or disco each week?   1 2 3 4 5 6 7

4. How many times do you clean your teeth each week?   1 2 3 4 5 6 7

Naturally it's very difficult to define who is a 'nominal Christian' and I am not sure we should really try. If we delve too deeply, we find that we can be accused of being 'nominal' on occasions. Anyway, we have to be careful that we are not doing what Jesus warned us about when he said, 'Take the log out of your own eye, and then you will be able to see clearly to take the speck out of your brother's eye' (see Matt. 7:1-5). But I wonder how other people do see us and how we see ourselves.

Action

Pass out paper and a pen for each person in your group and ask them to follow your instructions very carefully. As you give instructions, carry them out yourself. Use a board or large card so that your group can see clearly and understand. Block capitals should be used.

1. Write your date of birth in full in the middle of your page.
2. Write your full name underneath, trying to keep it central to the date of birth above.
3. Now underneath the name, write today's date.
4. Write down a word, phrase or very short sentence that describes you best (again, keeping it central).
5. Draw round what you have written, as shown (ie. as a tombstone).

Gradually there will be an awareness amongst the group of what they have done – drawn their own tombstone. And written their own epitaph. If we did die today, I wonder what God would want to put on our tombstones – does he see our faith as 'nominal'? Ultimately he can be the only judge. With God there can be no excuses. We cannot blame our circumstances for our failures. Nor can we say, as Albert Schweitzer once said: 'Men simply don't think.'

We must realise that this is very much a spiritual battle and we are constantly fighting against our natural desires, the expectations of people around us, and of course, the devil.

Bible Study

Turn in your Bibles to Galatians chapter 5 and read the whole chapter.

1. Christ has given us freedom (1). From what? What does it mean to stand firm?

2. How can we safeguard our freedom, and what keeps us from nominality? (13,7,8).

3. The Christian who wants to succeed should . . . (14,15). Nominality tends to keep spiritual truths as theories. So how can we practically see the outworking of these verses?

4. Verses 16-21 talk about the desires of the flesh. Again be practical – list each of these (19-21) and work out in which ways these affect us and make us nominal or ineffective.

5. The fruit of the Spirit, which in itself is contrary to nominality, is listed (22,23), but what does verse 25 mean?

Summary

● The nominal Christian, then, is somebody who does not really BELIEVE what God says. eg. ' I understand what the Bible says but . . . '

● The Spirit-filled Christian says 'I believe the Bible and on the basis of that I will think and do what is expected of me, with God's help'.

17ᵗʰ June 1959
Robert Moffett
16ᵗʰ January 1984
'Determined'

Building bigger biceps

Do you have a 'body beautiful'? Are you well proportioned in all the right places?

Are you bright, intelligent and doing well in your studies? Are you popular with everyone at home, school or work? Do you have a great spiritual life? Have you got the subjects of God, life, the universe and everything all sewn up?

If you answered 'yes' to all the above questions, come and tell me how you did it! If you did *not* answer 'yes' to the above questions, read on.

Development was one of the main themes of 'International Youth Year'. The term covers development at a national level, eg. technical progress in Third World countries, but it also covers personal development at the spiritual, mental, social and physical levels.

Unfortunately, some of the views on personal development expressed in an IYY publication 'Spark' could confuse rather than help us in our understanding of personal development. For example:
● 'It is realising that you are your own master and you can believe and think what you like'.
● 'We can all learn from each other – black and white, straight and gay, female and male – so start to get together to work for change'.

As Christians, we obviously believe in personal development but we don't believe that we are our own masters nor do we believe we can develop from views which are anti-biblical.

So for this session we're looking at building bigger social, physical, mental and spiritual biceps.

A Balanced Life

As human beings we are more than spiritual souls on two legs – we are religious, physical, social and mental creatures and we are different from animals.

Working it through

Stage One: Pass out duplicates or photocopies of the chart titled: 'Working it through'. Your group should tick the boxes next to the statements which apply to them and fill in the spaces if applicable.

The sheets they complete are theirs and will not be shown to anyone. You should tell them this when you pass the sheets out.

Stage Two: After completion they should make a priority list from the boxes they've ticked which outlines the main problems in their personal development.

Stage Three: Read together 2 Peter 1:3-9 and list together the ways, and means, by which God wishes us to develop personally.

Remind your group that Jesus was fully human as well as fully God, (John 1:14) and knows what it is like to be truly human. In our development, then, we are called to strive to be more like Jesus (Romans 8:28-30).

Stage Four: Ask your group to complete a final sheet entitled 'Changes'. In light of their priorities list and the verses they have looked up, what changes need to be made? Ask them to be practical. It may mean writing on their sheet 'see . . . (name of someone) who can help me sort this one out'. They need to make one 'change' for each 'priority'.

Working it through

1. Tick the boxes next to the statements which apply to you. Complete the sentences where applicable.
2. Number the major problems for you, in priority order.

Religious

☐ I don't agree with some things in the Bible.

☐ I'm not sure what God wants me to do in my life.

☐ I don't feel very close to God.

☐ I don't know what to say when people ask me what a Christian is.

☐ I'm scared stiff of sharing my faith.

☐ I find prayer and Bible study difficult.

☐ I think God is _____

☐ The word I would use to describe church is _____

☐ My parents make me go to church.

Social

☐ What can I do to get my mind off _____ ?

☐ I often like _____ _____, but I'm not sure that I should.

☐ I want people to like me.

☐ My friends put pressure on me to conform.

☐ I wish I had more fashionable clothes.

☐ I wish I had a really good friend to confide in.

☐ I don't like going along with my friends when they _____

☐ My parents are always arguing.

☐ I wish my parents understood me, particularly when _____

Physical

☐ I wish I looked better.

☐ I wish I looked like _____

☐ I wish I were better at sports.

☐ I can't get a girl/boyfriend.

☐ I don't think I will ever get married.

☐ How far should I go on a date?

☐ I wish I could lose weight.

☐ I wish I were as fit as _____

☐ If I were fit I would _____

Mental

☐ I feel guilty about _____

☐ My thoughts on _____ drive me crazy.

☐ I wish I were more intelligent.

☐ I wish I was as bright as _____

☐ I don't understand _____

☐ I wish I could talk to _____ about _____

☐ I think I'm going to fail my exams.

☐ I wish I could leave school.

☐ My teachers expect too much from me.

☐ I can't discipline myself.

26 *My philosophy of life*

Very few of us develop our own philosophy on life. We may think we do, without realising that our behaviour, reactions and opinions are often partly determined for us.

The role we play in the family affects us, the group of friends we associate with influences our views, and our general disposition (whether we're happy, sad, optimistic) will affect the way we react to situations in life.

Apart from these factors which affect the way we live our lives, we get life philosophies handed to us wholesale in books, magazines, newspapers, the theatre and music – particularly pop music.

In Jesus, though, we are set free to live life abundantly. Our family, friends and position in society and prevailing trendy philosophies *may* affect us but they don't *have* to determine the way we live our lives.

This Power Page is a role-playing game which looks at what life is like when our character and behaviour are dictated to us.

Programme

Begin by giving some introductory remarks about 'modern philosophers' using as examples the outlook on life that is presented by a few, selected pop groups. (Some of the more clued-up in your group might help you prepare this – or, at least, might lend you some records!) Then play 'Life is but a game'.

Life is but a game

Equipment

1. Large die made out of a cardboard box covered in paper. On each side is written a situation, e.g. 'On holiday', 'At a rock concert'. (See box below for details.)
2. You will need to make forty-six cards of some kind (index cards would do). These are divided into four packs (see box for what to write on each card).

How to play

1. The game is a role play involving up to six players.
2. Each person draws a card from the pack marked 'family' which determines the role they will play in the game. They may tell each other their character. Players then draw one card each from the remaining packs which determines their personality, attitude and position in society. They must not show the other players their cards.
3. The cube is then rolled and the side facing upwards determines the situation in which the role play takes place.
4. Allow three minutes for discussion in which players can work out a rough story outline if they want and decide who's going to start the game off.

Cube situations

A riotous party

A shopping expedition

A classical concert

A pop concert

A police station

On holiday

Personality cards

You get angry easily

You are frustrated

You are depressed

You are placid

You are well-liked

You are patient

You are friendly

You are content

You are greedy

You are caring

You are selfish

You are crude

You are prayerful

You are happy-go-lucky

You are generous

Attitude cards

You love music

You have a sports car

You are a communist

You enjoy parties

You dislike work

You spend a high proportion of your money on clothes

You are a Christian

You work hard

You are very studious

You enjoy eating out at good and expensive restaurants

You have very little money

You enjoy travelling

You are a Conservative

You are highly intelligent

You enjoy watching TV

Position cards

Factory worker

Shop Assistant

Unemployed

Police Officer

Student

Teacher Training

Bank Clerk

Computer Operator

Family cards

MUM

DAD

DAUGHTER (19)

SON (18)

DAUGHTER (24) MARRIED

SON-IN-LAW (26)

For example, a player acting the daughter role who has drawn cards saying she is depressed and a shop assistant with very little money might start off a scene on a shopping expedition with: 'Good grief, Mum, I don't know where these young girls today get the money to buy all these new fashions. I've hardly got enough to pay the rent'. Mum must then respond according to the character she's playing.

5. After four minutes, and when every player has had a chance to speak, get people to discuss the role play and guess what kind of character each player was playing.

Debriefing

Go on to discuss what values each player seemed to have – what or who was important to them in life, and why? Does anyone recognise these role-play values as being their own in real life? Were any of the values/philosophies of life inadequate, inconsistent . . ? Which ones were worth imitating? Why?

Jesus principles

Discuss with the group the Bible's philosophy on life by looking at the 'Jesus Principles' listed below.
- John 17:14-18
- John 10:9,10
- 1 Corinthians 6:19,20
- Ephesians 4:20-32
- James 5:1-6
- James 3:13-18

Planning ahead

Christians are lousy planners! Some of the more enlightened seem to be able to survive with just a twenty-four-hour day.

Others stumble from one crisis to another ... even to the point of enjoying it. But most of us see a week go by and see another looming in front of us and ask what it's all about.

I never have any time to do all the things I want to do and when I do, I do them all in such a rush that I don't enjoy them.

Your average youth member may not share your pre-occupation with time-management. He or she may be so *laissez-faire* about life that the nearest they get to planning for the future is wondering what to wear at the next party.

This Power Page takes a look at planning and organising your time.

Set the scene

As people arrive in your home (or wherever you hold your meeting) plan *not* to have things ready, e.g., have the vacuum cleaner out, be washing up, have the telephone ringing, arrange for the speaker for next week to turn up and be turned away – perhaps your minister.

Plan to be so disorganised that you can't find the props or equipment you need for games and activities. Really go over the top so that it is a disaster. This will work well as long as this is *not* your normal state.

● Alternatively, arrive and just sit there for ten minutes apologising because you had no time to plan or prepare anything and you don't know what to do. Watch the interplay of embarrassment among group members and then watch and see who in the group does something to fill the vacuum.

An important lesson for you and your group to discover is that whenever you plan a vacuum or allow one to occur, people and situations will always fill it for you.

Activity

Announce that you are looking at the subject of 'planning'.

Ask the group to complete an hour-by-hour time sheet of what they did over the last twenty-four hours and also mornings, afternoons and evenings over the last week. Read out *your* schedule but tell them in advance that their schedule is confidential.

Bible study

Show how Jesus and Paul organised their time:
● Jesus planned his day – Mark 1:21-45 (twenty-four hours in the life of Jesus)
● His schedule – Mark 11:1-11, 15-19; 3:13-19
● Paul planned his itinerary – Acts 13:1-3; 13:13-14

Planning ahead

Get your group to make up their own schedule in which they plan carefully what they propose to do the following week. They should not expect to follow it every moment of the day but see it as a guideline. They should ask God to help them discover which priorities are in God's mind, and then place them in a 'week plan'.

As the leader, you should make a list of examples of activities which should be included in their timesheets, e.g: homework, prayer, Bible reading, TV, socialising (dating), youth group, etc.

Tell your group that when you have completed yours, you're going to pin it up for them to see!
Keep the evening light but show the necessity very clearly for planning. What's more, don't be afraid to do the exercise yourself.

Week plan

DAY	ACTIVITY		
	am	pm	evening
MONDAY			
TUESDAY	Washing		
WEDNESDAY			
THURSDAY		Housegroup planning	Housegroup
FRIDAY		Shop	
SATURDAY			
SUNDAY			

SPECIAL OCCASIONS

28

Easter Peace

Qui desiderat pacem, praeparet bellum.

('Let him who desires peace prepare for war' – that's the meaning of the above Latin quote from the fourth-century writer Vegetius.)

The organisers of International Youth Year called for peace education at a personal, community and international level.

To quote from an IYY publication: 'One of the most important ways to start to work for peace is simply to think about it. Why do the super powers have enough weapons to destroy the world fifty times over? Why does someone starve to death on average every seven seconds? Peace education can start to provide some of the reasons and suggest some of the answers'.

What absolute twaddle. Peace can only come about in the biblical sense by a change of heart.

Action

Send two people out the week before the meeting to accost people in the streets with two simple questions: 'What does the word "peace" mean to you? And how can we achieve it?' They should tape the answers as they are given. Ask them to edit the tape so that they have five minutes of good interviewing.

Set up your meeting in the normal Moffett manner so that the room atmosphere has some connection with the discussion topic. However, you should try to create the opposite atmosphere to peace.

For example, if you are having your meeting in a house with a telephone, you should encourage three or four friends to telephone within the first three minutes of your start to the meeting with at least two people calling in, and others shouting

at the cat or dog. I hope you've got the picture; but now exaggerate it.

Begin by playing the tape. On finishing, throw magazines of all types, including teenage periodicals, into the middle of the floor, along with scissors, glue, string, wood and card.

Explain to your group that you want them to make a collage on the subject of what peace means to them. They can cut their card to a particular shape if they like. Give

them 16 minutes to do this.

Ask a few of the group to volunteer their explanation for the use of their pictures (and shape of card) etc. Draw out of them their deepest feelings about personal as well as world peace.

Research

Split your group into small units and ask them to answer the following questions on peace.

PEACE
(20th Century Version)

Questions on Peace

1. What should be the content and goal of all Christian preaching? (Eph. 6:15; Acts 10:36; Eph. 2:1, 14-17)
2. How can peace be established? (1 Cor. 14:33; Rom. 15:33)
3. How do we find this peace with God? (Rom. 5:1; Col. 1:19,20)
4. Who gives this peace? Can we find it from within ourselves? (Rom. 1:7; 1 Cor. 1:3; 2 Thess. 3:16)

Read the following comment about peace to your group:

'Peace in the Old Testament and the New Testament is not seen purely as an opposite to war. Sadly that's the way we usually see it today. No, it's much more. When God offers his peace, or when we offer peace to other people we are asking for God's very best that is possible for that person. It is a sense of God's presence and purpose in our lives giving us a sense of acceptance and contentedness in spite of the turmoil and pressure around us.'

Easter

Easter is the highlight of the year for Christians. It is this time when we remember that Christ gave us peace with God because of his death and resurrection.

It is an important time when we celebrate his passion, because his act of supreme suffering has given us a new life of peace (2 Cor. 5:17).

May I suggest that in your church, before taking communion, you walk around (as they do in Anglican churches) before the actual giving of the bread and wine and shake one another's hand (or embrace them depending on how British you are) and offer them God's peace – his shalom – his very, very best for their lives.

Finally, read carefully and quietly John 14:27-31 and leave a few moments of silence for prayer.

Story time

● Many years ago there was a king who offered a great deal of gold to the artist who could paint the best picture of peace to decorate the main palace hall. Many artists produced wonderful paintings.

The king sorted out two which he really liked but he had to choose between them. One picture was of a calm lake which reflected the peaceful towering mountains all around it and, for all but one small fluffy cloud, a beautiful, clear, blue sky. All who saw this picture thought that it was a perfect image of peace.

The other picture also had mountains but of a very different nature. These were rugged and bare and looked far from peaceful in the midst of a storm with lightning across the sky. A waterfall gushed down the side of one of the mountains.

The king looked and looked, then he noticed behind the gushing waterfall a tiny bush which was growing in a crack in the rock. In the bush was a bird on her nest, sitting amongst all the turmoil of the wind and noise of the storm. Sitting in perfect peace.

The king chose the painter of the second picture as the winner of the gold. Why? 'Because', said the king, 'peace is not being in a place where there is no confusion or hard work or trouble. Peace is to be amongst these things and yet know calmness in the turmoil around us. This is the real meaning of peace'.

29 *Christmas foot party*

I have always believed that laughter, as well as being a good healer, is often a good form of communicating something important.

As Christmas approaches, most people think of parties – and I think of feet!! I don't know why, except that feet are perhaps one of the most humorous aspects of our bodies. So here we go . . . with a *Power Pack* 'foot party'.

Action

Organise your evening to give a party atmosphere, with food, music, decorations, etc. Preferably, hold your meeting in a house. If you can go as far as to use 'feet' as your theme with the food, decor and music, even better.

As your group arrives, everybody must undress their feet. No undressing – no entry! Play the majority of these games:

Feet Fancy Dress

Like any beauty or fancy dress contest, line up your 'feet' parade together as a group. Then look at each contestant individually. Finally, hold 'feet' interviews. Bring in members from your church to announce the winners. (Choose those who would not feel inhibited about such a display of indecency!)

Feet Signature

Give each foot-owner one minute to get as many signatures on one foot as possible. When the minute is up, go around and count them. Don't forget the odd tickle!

Toe Wrestling

Couples lie on their backs with their feet facing each other. The couple then lock their toes and, on a signal, try and pin each others' toes to the ground. (Like arm wrestling but using 'piggies' instead!)

Preparation

Prior to the meeting, arrange for posters to be placed in prominent positions around the church premises, and other places where your group hang out. Arrange for your 'Foot Party' to be announced as many times as possible in the church.

The posters should give the emphasis that bare feet will be required and that girls should be wearing jeans/trousers. Make it clear that there will be a 'no option' fancy dress contest and that they should come prepared to attire their feet in suitable 'fancy dress'. Have a picture on your poster of a foot in 'fancy dress'.

eet Beauty Contest
ke the 'fancy dress' competition
xcept that you give prizes for:
rettiest feet; biggest toe nail;
iggest small toe; most shapely
oot; etc.

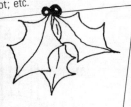

Feet Jumble
This is one of my favourites – a camera is a 'must'! Choose five people and ask them to lie on the floor side by side with their feet in a straight line. Write in felt tip pen one letter on each foot which, when put in the right order spell 'Smelly Feet'; for example the letters in the wrong order might read LTEFELYSME. Ask one person to re-arrange the feet in the correct order with the rule that everybody remains where they are positioned. This is an unbelievable sight! It's agony!

oot-pass Orange
wo equal and mixed lines of people
ass an orange using only their feet.
f the orange touches the ground they
tart again. Of course, the winning
eam is the one who pass it from one
end to the other first.

Foot Measure
Again, using two mixed teams, ask contestants to line their 'right' feet up to each other, toe to heel. The winning team is the one with the biggest 'footage'. Do the same with the 'left' feet to see if there is a difference – you may get a surprise.

Vine Making
lace some grapes in two bowls.
have two lads compete to see who
an make the most juice with his
are feet. Pour the juice into jars to
measure the winner. Then the loser
drinks the winner's juice!

Break for some eats and drinks.

Now have a Christmas 'Footalogue'
Read the story of Christmas from Luke 2:1-7, explaining very briefly that Jesus humbled himself. Even though he was God, he became man and came in a very lowly way as a baby, born in a smelly stable. He took upon himself the role of a servant, and demonstrated this aspect of the Christmas story right through to his death.

Read John 13:1-5. Jesus showed the real meaning of his incarnation (his coming among us) in this story. This particular incident may well have been the time when the disciples were arguing as to who was going to be the greatest (Luke 22:24).

As Christians, the Christmas story is about humility and servanthood. No disciple of any rabbi would have stooped that low and washed the feet of his master – it was the duty of the lowest slave to wash the feet of a master.

Bring out a bowl of water and a towel and, with all seriousness, take steps to wash the feet of all your youth group. At the end someone may wash yours – but let that happen naturally.

Finish by singing some choruses and carols that reflect the mood and subject of the evening. 'For unto us a child is born, to us a son is given.'

A Christmas cracker

After weeks of cards, tinsel and TV advertising, Christmas finally arrives.

But this outline isn't going to knock commercialism or make us feel guilty by talking about poverty while we eat Christmas dinner. Instead we're going to celebrate Christmas in style.

Besides Easter, Christmas brings us the glorious message of new birth. So we are going to toast the occasion with plenty of fun. Good planning will make this a fantastic evening – not to be forgotten.

Preparation

Contact all your youth group well before the meeting, inviting any lapsed members along too.

● Announce that you are going to have a Christmas celebration – give them the date and the time and ask them to bring along a wrapped present which has a meaningful Christmas message for whoever receives it, whether male or female. The only condition is that it should not cost more than 50p (excluding gift paper). Alternatively, people could wrap up the materials and instructions needed to make a Christmas present. The choice is theirs as long as it has a Christmas message. The present should not say who it is from or who it should go to.

● Arrange for plenty of food and drink and decorations. It is preferable to hold your 'celebration' in a home.

● Organise a group of your youngsters to practise some musical items: popular carols, appropriate choruses and Christmas songs (which could include children's songs). Make sure that you have enough books or sheets so that everyone can join in – never assume that everyone knows the carols.

● Give some of your group members a week's notice to prepare written monologues of three minutes' length. Each person should take on one of the following Bible characters telling in his or her own words what they saw and felt. The Bible references are alongside so they can get a feel for the story. It should be humorous as well as serious. They must use their imagination a bit.

For example, a few opening lines that the innkeeper might say: 'Yeh, well it was one of those busy nights. I felt a bit bad turning them away like . . . young couple with her about to "produce" any minute.

'The last thing I wanted to was to 'ave to run around with 'ot water an' all that when I've got me customers to look after. Anyway it weren't my fault I couldn't 'elp. It was Augustus' fault (spit) – 'e wanted the census didn't he . . . so me an' my missus decided that . . .' etc.

● Work out some creative games for the evening (see the book 'Crowdbreakers' – by Bob Moffett, published by Pickering Paperbacks).

● Ask one of your more technically-minded youth to get five or six one-minute taped interviews with young children on what Christmas means to them. They could do this by going into the Sunday school the week before.

Programme
I would suggest that your evening lasts anything from two to two-and-a-half hours in all – a Christmas bonanza indeed!

Monologues
● **Joseph,** when he heard Mary was pregnant (Matt. 1:18-25).
● **Mary,** when the angel appeared to her (Luke 1:26-38).
● **Elizabeth,** on hearing Mary's news (Luke 1:39-45).
● **One of the Shepherds,** after the angel's visit (Luke 2:8-20).
● **The Innkeeper,** after the birth (Luke 2:1-7).
● **One of the Visitors from the East** (Matt. 2:1-12).
● **Herod** (Matt. 2:1-18).
● **Mary,** on the killing of the innocents (Matt. 2:16).
● **The Angel Gabriel and Friends** (Luke 1:26-38; 2:8-14).

Why not . . . ?
1. Go carol singing and monologuing around elderly people's and children's homes.
2. Go carol singing around the streets. Instead of collecting money, give a suitable piece of Christmas or gospel literature to them when they open the door. Watch their faces as you refuse any attempt to give you money.
3. Have a 'Scrooge Drive', where you gather tins of food from the community to give to the poorer members of the area.
4. Go carol singing in the shopping area, again giving out literature.
5. If you did the session on the elderly (number 5), don't forget the elderly folk you 'adopted' then.

Suggestions
1. Crazy games to get everyone mixing. See the games in the book 'Crowdbreakers' Nos. 2-6.
2. Singing.
3. Short prayers.
4. Children's ideas of Christmas (tape).
5. Children's Christmas songs, eg. 'I saw three ships come sailing in . . .'
6. Food: Do this by numbering people 1, 2, 3, 4, 5, 6 etc. so that number 1 has to get food for number 2; 3 has to get food for 4 etc. The even numbers have to communicate what they want all at the same time as the 'odd' numbers hussle together to get what is required. Then the roles (not rolls) are reversed so that 'evens' get the orders of the odds.
7. Singing and musical items (a little more serious) interspersed with monologues (you choose the order).
8. Presents: As the leader, prepare a short speech declaring why we give presents at Christmas. Then with all seriousness ask your odds to go and get a present for their evens and vice versa. Presents should be neatly stacked beforehand on a table.
9. Communion: If appropriate you may wish to hold a very simple service of communion at this point.
10. Singing and prayer: Finish with some quiet and meaningful songs.

Love: actions and feelings

No one fully understands 'love' except for God. He is love and knows what it means.

Love is something which is outward going and can never be restrained. In 1 Corinthians 13 Paul has a go at trying to describe what love is but it is only an attempt and Paul struggles to express his thoughts in that passage of the Bible.

Love is not only an action it is also feelings, and who can describe objectively to someone else such deep and inward emotions?

At Christmas time we remember that 'God so loved the world . . . that he gave his only Son . . .' (John 3:16). So this page is an attempt to deepen our understanding of love.

Sketches

Decide on someone's home for this meeting providing all the necessary things required to give it a festive atmosphere: food, last years' Christmas cards, and decorations.

The Four Loves

C S Lewis made famous the four different types of love found and expressed in the Bible. Briefly summarise the four different loves, as described below, and tell your group about them.

Love of Friends
(Greek: *philia*)
A concept often misunderstood in our society today. Philia is a very deep friendship between people that is based on mutual interests and loyalty. Often this love is closely associated with agápe love.

Affectionate Love
(*Storge*)
This kind of love is a very general 'sentimental' feeling for people and things. On one level it can be the love of a parent and a child but it can also be a feeling for places we have lived in, favourite clothes that we do not like to give up, etc.

It is an affection that can exist between say, a very young man and an old lady of a very different status. The love allows tolerance between pupils in a class; neighbours next door, etc.

Sexual Love
(*Eros*)
This is the love that declares 'I have fallen in love'. It manifests itself in very strong feelings and emotions towards a person of the opposite sex coupled with a very strong physical attraction.

It would generally be true to say that girls tend towards the former and boys the latter.

Christian Love
(*Agape*)
This is the highest form of love. It means accepting the other person(s) for what they are and being prepared to secure their greatest happiness and joy at one's own expense. The

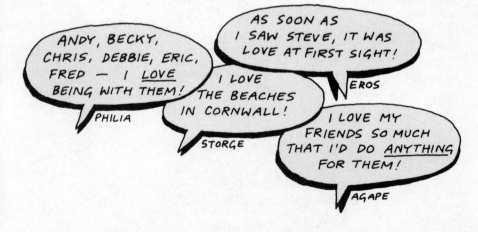

ultimate form of this love is found in the words of Jesus: 'The greatest love a person can have for his friends is to give his life for them'.

Now split your group into four and ask them to provide a sketch to last no more than four minutes on one of the following which you will designate.

1. A group of friends meeting to plan a surprise Christmas party for Jenny and her mother. Jenny's father died three months ago.

2. A son or daughter discussing plans with a parent about their Christmas trip to London to work with the down and outs. The son or daughter is seeking advice.

3. At Pete's Christmas party some of the lads try and chat up the girls.

4. At Jenny's Christmas party, Sara notices that Julia, who is disabled, has not yet turned up. Even though it is at the height of the party, Sara quietly leaves to find out if Julia is OK and whether she wants some help getting to the party.

Discuss the different 'loves' involved in the sketches so that each person can grasp the meaning of the loves shown in the Bible.

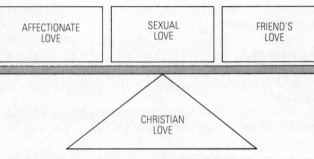

Bible time

In the four different groups ask them to look at the biblical examples of the four loves. Each group takes one example.

● **Love of Friends:** 1 Samuel 19 and 20.
● **Affectionate Love:** Genesis 45.
● **Sexual Love:** 2 Samuel 11.
● **Christian Love:** John 15:13 and John 19.

They should answer the following questions:

1. Who is showing the particular love(s) and what type?
2. What reaction is this love(s) creating?
3. What can we learn from this love(s)?

Show your group the diagram and very briefly explain that it is the agape love that keeps all our other loves in balance – it is the 'fulcrum'.

Letter time

Ask each member of your group to write a Christmas card to God asking for forgiveness for their bad relationships and telling God how they are going to change.

As the leader you should purchase the cards and envelopes.

Give them the choice as to whether they give you the cards or, better, keep them themselves.

Togetherness

Read Luke 2:1-7 together in a meditative way, that is, allowing a few moments' silence after each verse. Invite people to pray and sing choruses or to reflect upon the evening.

Facing fear at New Year

Another year . . . but what is going to happen to me?

Is someone in my family going to die?

Am I going to pass those examinations this summer? Will my parents split up this year? Will my girlfriend marry me?

'Verbophobia' is the fear of words. Will I have enough words and ideas for this Power Page? Fear is debilitating. It can bring depression, failure and jealousy.

This page will help your youth group to face these issues.

Quiz

In a very relaxed way, ask the group as a whole what the following technical terms mean. They are all types of fear.

- **Acrophobia** – fear of heights.
- **Aerophobia** – fear of flying.
- **Agoraphobia** – fear of open spaces.
- **Androphobia** – fear of men.
- **Aquaphobia** – fear of water.
- **Autophobia** – fear of being alone.
- **Botanophobia** – fear of plants.
- **Decidophobia** – fear of making decisions.
- **Ergophobia** – fear of work.
- **Gynephobia** – fear of women.
- **Necrophobia** – fear of dead bodies.
- **Nucleophobia** – fear of nuclear bombs.
- **Ochlophobia** – fear of crowds.
- **Phobophobia** – fear of one's own fears.
- **Technophobia** – fear of technology.
- **Zoophobia** – fear of animals.

SCALPOPHOBIA: FEAR OF HAIRCUTS

Group activity

Give each person a pen and paper and ask them to make up a word for their own fears.

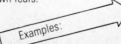

Examples:

- **Examinophobia** – fear of exams.
- **Firaphobia** – fear of fires.
- **Phoniaphobia** – fear of telephones.
- **Orientophobia** – fear of Orient Football Club losing, or of travelling to the middle east.

Read out the good ones, unless some of them are too personal. Suggest that some of the more comical ones go into the church or youth club magazine.

Special guest evening
Arrange for four people from very different walks of life to come and talk about their fears. This is done by putting them in 'the hot seat' and by asking them deep, penetrating questions about their fears.

If you really want to go over the top (as I would) you will point a spot-light into the visitor's face with complete darkness all around. Get young and old alike to take part – ask questions about day-to-day things. It's worth asking people from outside your church to come – ask your minister for contacts. Make sure he is the first on your visitors' list.

Split your group into smaller units and get them to answer the following quiz.

Quizansphobia
1. Why do we fear the future?
2. Why is it that we sometimes fear people?
3. Why do we fear failure?
4. Why is the dark seen as such a fearful thing?

Summing up
As Christians, we may often be placed in fearful circumstances. It is what we do with our fear that is important. In 1 John 4:18, we read that God's 'perfect love drives out fear.'

We need to learn that we can trust in God whatever fear is around us. Something to be learnt! Arrange for four people to read the following verses at the end.

What others say about fear
● **King David:** Psalm 34:1-8.
● **Fear of the future:** Ecclesiastes 12:1-5.
● **Peter:** 1 Peter 5:7.
● **Jesus:** Matthew 6:34; John 16:33.

Important! As it is the beginning of a new year ask the members of your group to write a letter to God telling him about their fears for the new year. Then ask them to write John 16:33 at the bottom.

Give them good writing paper and envelopes. Then ask for the letters, in sealed envelopes with their own name on, saying that you will give them back at the end of the year. Make sure you remember to do this!

33 Valentine's Day

It comes once each year, so here are some ideas for coping with relationships. ('Relationships' is the Christian word for dating and romance.)

'Dating' is a relatively new thing. Before 1200 AD it was almost unheard of. Even today in some cultures marriages are still arranged by the parents. Although many of us would resist that concept, there are many such couples who learn to love each other and have very caring and stable marriages.

Getting a correct attitude to dating, early on, can save some of the heartaches and disasters of adolescent relationships which often hinder us in later life.

So, Valentines – this is for you!

Action

Prepare your evening by choosing a suitable room and trying to give it a romantic effect with soft lights and music. Ask your group to come reasonably dressed up for the evening.

Intermingle your activities with food and suitable drinks, eg. mix up some cordial drinks, add some tonic water and call it a special 'passion' drink. Hopefully, it will not taste too unpalatable.

Start by playing some 'dating' Crowdbreakers. I suggest the following games but if you wish to choose more then see 'Crowdbreakers' numbers 23, 31 and 59.

Descriptive partners: Each guy is introduced to a girl and asked to write a description of this girl as he sees her, but without stating her name. He must not refer to the colours of her clothes as this will be too obvious.

When everyone has completed this task, all the slips are collected and mixed up in a bowl. Then each guy selects a slip and must find the girl he thinks fits the description.

You can vary the game by having the guys draw pictures of the girls or by having the girls describe the boys.

Caution: For obvious reasons you must know your group very well for this one to go right and not give offence.

Dating attitudes

1. When you were 10 years old, what was your opinion of the opposite sex? Has it changed? Why?

2. How would you react if one day your parents announced to you that you were going to marry a son (daughter) of one of their friends; someone you didn't know at all?

Tick where appropriate
3. I look upon dating as:
- ☐ a) part of growing up
- ☐ b) having a good time
- ☐ c) an opportunity to develop friendships
- ☐ d) something I am expected to do
- ☐ e) unnecessary
- ☐ f) a way of sorting out my ideas about the opposite sex
- ☐ g) preparation for marriage
- ☐ h) discovering my sexual desires
- ☐ i) a way of getting out of the house
- ☐ j) other (please specify)

4. The most difficult thing about dating is:
- ☐ a) asking someone out
- ☐ b) deciding where to go
- ☐ c) waiting to get that letter or phone call
- ☐ d) making conversation
- ☐ e) what my friends say if they see me
- ☐ f) ordering drinks or meals
- ☐ g) controlling my sexual desire
- ☐ h) knowing how to say goodnight
- ☐ i) knowing how to say goodbye
- ☐ j) finding money for the date
- ☐ k) what my parents are going to say
- ☐ l) trying to get my homework done in time

5. My idea of a date is (*no **more** than 51 words, no **less** than 34 words*):

6. My friends think that my attitude to dating is (*no **more** than 14 words*):

Balloon hugging: Select couples, who are each given three balloons. On the signal to start, the couple must blow up the three balloons and place two of the balloons under the girl's armpits and have her sit on the third. The guy tries to burst the balloons by hugging the girl. The winning couple is the first to burst the three balloons. (This one has got to be seen to be believed.)

Mr and Mrs: Select four couples who have been going out together for some time. The guys are then asked to leave the room while a set of questions is put to the girls. Ask questions like 'Where did you go for your first date?' 'What was the first thing he ever gave you?' 'When it comes to spending money, what word best describes him?' The guys are then brought back and asked the same questions. Couples receive points for similar answers. This can be very good if well prepared, imaginative questions and option answers are used.

Pass out paper with the following questions on 'Dating attitudes' on it. Ask them to complete the questions totally by themselves. I suggest that you give them 16 minutes to complete the page and then gently, with humour and a taint of seriousness, ask for answers (on a voluntary basis). One other way of getting information is to gather the sheets and read out the answers for each section. But anonymity must be paramount.

Finally, as a group discuss the following guidelines that the Bible suggests for interpersonal relationships, ie. how we should perceive, and relate to, others.

● Make a list of some qualities you would look for in a dating partner. Now compare your list with 1 Samuel 16:7 and 1 Peter 3:3,4. What does 1 Peter 3:4 mean?

● What five things does the Bible say about our relationships with unbelievers, in terms of marriage (2 Cor. 6:14-16)? Are these guidelines ones that we should take seriously in dating?

● Where do we fit parents into our thinking about dating? See Ephesians 6:1-4 and Colossians 3:20. Make a list of guidelines for yourself of how you are going to react to dating problems, as a result of these verses.